INDIAN MENUS

A New One, Everyday!

For my husband,
who has been my inspiration all through ...

Published 2002 by
Rupa & Co
7/16, Ansari Road, Daryaganj
New Delhi 110 002

Sales Centres:
Allahabad Bangalore Chandigarh Chennai
Dehradun Hyderabad Jaipur Kathmandu
Kolkata Ludhiana Mumbai Pune

ISBN 81-7167-860-2

Photographs: Namas Bhujani

Design & Typset: Arrt Creations
45 Nehru Apts, Kalkaji
New Delhi 110 019

Printed in India by
Gopsons Papers Ltd
A-14 Sector 60
Noida 201 301

INDIAN MENUS

A New One, Everyday!

Malti Jindal

Foreword

F E R O Z   K H A N

Rupa & Co

Acknowledgements

Firstly, I would like to thank my husband, Deepak, without whose support and encouragement I could have never written this book. I would like to thank my mother Pushpa Agarwal, who was my real mentor and taught me all the skills I have acquired, and my father, M K Agarwal, without whom I could have never made this book a reality. My parents-in-law, Saroj and S N Jindal have been a source of inspiration all through. My daughters — Chandni, Twinkle and Karishma, have always been there to appreciate, support and cheer me. My dear friend, connoisseur and advisor, Feroz Khan, without whose constant comments and praise of whatever I prepared for him, I would have never realised this dream.

My friend Kiran Melwani, whose words of encouragement and appreciation gave me the freedom to experiment.

I would like to thank Sangeeta, who painstakingly typed these recipes out.

I would like to thank my publishers, Rupa & Co., for the effort they have made. My heartfelt thanks to Arundhati Nag and Jayapriya Vasudevan of Jacaranda Press.

Lastly, my heart goes out to my large family and numerous friends who have made the experience of cooking worthwhile.

CONTENTS

FOREWORD

If one has faith in the saying, "The way to a man's heart is through his stomach", Malti has won over many hearts and certainly my admiration and tastebuds. What is unique about her talent is the swiftness and speed with which she prepares cuisines of different regions and varieties. Dishing out a complete meal for eight or ten people takes her as little as an hour-and-a-half. Over the years that I have known her, I have been impressed by her art of whipping up a great meal without spending several tiresome hours in the kitchen.

I strongly believe that we were born herbivores; if God wanted us to be carnivores, I am sure we would have been endowed with a pair of large canines! I recommend all food enthusiasts to explore the huge and unexplored arena of vegetarian cuisine. Malti has opened up a whole new world of healthy and delicious Indian vegetarian recipes for all of us to devour.

When I work feverishly on a script or when I am thick in the middle of filming, I prefer being alone, cooking my own meals. I remember many occasions, when I have called Malti and asked her to give me easy-to-prepare recipes for wholesome meals to take me through those frenzied days.

I find cooking an immensely relaxing exercise. In my farmhouse, on the outskirts of Bangalore, I have deliberately built two kitchens — one for my staff and the other which is my personal and private sanctum, is where I experiment with different kinds of food ideas. Malti has been instrumental in helping me set up this kitchen and constantly provides me with new and innovative recipes, which I try out with gusto.

Feroz Khan

INTRODUCTION

In a country as diverse as India, it would be surprising if the culinary history wasn't as rich and varied as its culture. Each region has a heritage of cuisines with smells, aromas and cooking styles uniquely peculiar to its geographic location, climate, lifestyle and tastebuds. In the cold reaches of the Himalayas in the North, saffron is used widely in cooking as it helps keep the body warm; in the deserts of Rajasthan, the luscious red chilli is used extensively as it has hydrating powers; the abundant growth of coconut trees in the coastal South contributes to its cooking being rich with the delicate flavours of coconut powder and spices. This book attempts to bring together the various cuisines of India in order to give the reader a feel of the vastness of our gastronomic map.

The unique aspect of this book is that I have tried to put together a book of menus rather than a straightforward compilation of recipes. I have created a 30-day menu planner by which readers can plan a special meal, every day of the month.

The most important ingredient of cooking a good meal is perhaps the love one invests while planning, preparing and serving it. When I whip up meals for my family and friends, I sometimes try to add a special touch or sudden innovative spice to my dishes, apart from the ones listed in the recipe. Cooking is an intensely personal experience for me and seeing people I love relish the food I have cooked, is satisfaction enough.

I learnt to cook when I was a child of ten. My most excited hours were spent in watching my mother pottering in the kitchen — grinding aromatic spices, supervising the consistency of her *dals* and curries, checking the delicate seasonings which would crackle on the simmering fires. Fortunately for me, my family encouraged my initial forays into the intricate web of culinary land, never once disheartening my first tentative and sometimes even disastrous ventures!

I am immensely grateful to my husband, friends and relatives who have tasted my food and commented like connoisseurs and indeed have encouraged me to try new techniques and conjure up novel dishes. My extensive travels in the West and Far East have helped me imbibe delicate flavours and translate them into reality in the privacy of my kitchen.

The recipes listed here are all vegetarian. They represent characteristics of the various regions of India, reflecting its rich diversity. All recipes cater to serving four people; for larger numbers, judge accordingly.

I have tried to add some spice and novelty for your palate by giving three menus comprising mouth-watering *chaats*. One doesn't always have to stick to the staid soup-salad-main course-cereal-dessert format. These *chaat* menus are for those lazy holidays when your taste buds are in the mood for a change.

In the end, I would like to emphasise the fact in cooking there is no 'right' or 'wrong' method. Every individual has his or her own particular method and style; the vastness of our country and its numerous communities lend it a myriad cooking techniques. The recipes I have given are the best ways I have known to prepare these dishes. If you have other ways of making the same, I am sure they too stand the test of tastebuds just as these have and are just as correct.

I hope all of you enjoy cooking these dishes as much as I did.

BASIC RECIPES

MILK PRODUCTS, CHUTNEYS AND SAUCES

Plain Curd/*Dahi*

Clarified Butter/*Ghee*

Cottage Cheese/*Paneer*

Wholemilk Fudge/*Khoya*

Tamarind Chutney/*Saunth*

Coriander Chutney

Mint Chutney

Coriander and Mint Chutney

Coconut Chutney

Onion and Tomato Chutney

Boiled Rice

Boiled Dal

Tomato Puree

White Sauce

CONDIMENTS

Garam Masala

Kashmiri Garam Masala

Rasam Powder

Sambhar Powder

PLAIN CURD/DAHI

INGREDIENTS

Milk	4 cups
Curd	1 tbsp

METHOD

1. Boil milk and let cool. When it is lukewarm, add 1 tbsp of curd and mix well. Cover and keep aside for 4-5 hours.
2. After 5 hours, refrigerate. Use as plain curd or to make *raitas*.

CLARIFIED BUTTER/GHEE

INGREDIENTS

Butter	500 gms

METHOD

1. Melt butter in a saucepan, then allow it to simmer until a clear yellow liquid is formed and a sediment settles on the base of the pan. This should take about 25 minutes.
2. Carefully strain the clarified butter through a muslin cloth, making sure that all the sediments have been removed. Pour into a container with a close-fitting cover.
3. When set, this milky-white or slightly yellow solid can be stored in a covered container for long periods without getting spoilt.

COTTAGE CHEESE/PANEER

INGREDIENTS

Milk	4 cups
Lemon juice	2 tbsp

METHOD

1. Bring the milk slowly to a boil. Gradually add the lemon juice, stirring continuously, until the milk curdles.
2. Set aside to cool, then strain the curdled milk through a muslin-lined sieve. Squeeze out the liquid (whey), then keep the *paneer* pressed under a heavy flat weight for at least an hour.
3. Cut into rectangular pieces or use as directed in the recipes.

WHOLEMILK FUDGE/KHOYA

INGREDIENTS

Milk	4 ½ cups

METHOD

1. Bring the milk to a boil in a large heavy-bottomed saucepan. Reduce heat and simmer, stirring frequently for about 40–45 minutes.
2. The milk should be reduced to about a quarter of its original volume. When ready, the *khoya* should resemble a ball of sticky dough. It is used for making Indian sweets or in rich curries.

TAMARIND CHUTNEY/SAUNTH

INGREDIENTS

Tamarind	1 cup (200 gms)
Jaggery	2 cups (100 gms)
Salt	to taste
Red chilli powder	1 tsp
Roasted cumin seed powder	1 tsp
Black salt	½ tsp
Garam masala powder	¾ tsp
Oil	1 tbsp
Cumin seeds	½ tsp

METHOD

1. Soak tamarind with jaggery overnight in 2 cups of water.

2.. Mash with hand and strain through a sieve.

3. Heat oil in a pan and add cumin seeds. When they turn brown, add the tamarind-jaggery mixture and all the spices. Boil and cook for 10 to 15 minutes.

4. Cool at room temperature and store in the refrigerator. Use when required.

Note: This chutney can be stored for one month in the refrigerator.

CORIANDER CHUTNEY

INGREDIENTS

Coriander leaves	1 bunch
Green chillies	4–5
Salt	to taste
Raw mango, peeled and chopped	1, small

METHOD

Mix all the ingredients and grind to a paste.

MINT CHUTNEY

INGREDIENTS

Mint leaves	2 bunches
Salt	to taste
Green chillies	4–5
Juice	of 2 lemons

METHOD

1.. Remove the leaves from the mint sticks and wash thoroughly.

2. Grind all the ingredients to a paste.

Note: This chutney can also be served, mixed with hung curd.

CORIANDER AND MINT CHUTNEY

INGREDIENTS

Coriander leaves	1 bunch
Mint leaves	1 bunch
Salt	to taste
Green chillies	3
Cumin seeds	1 tsp
Coriander powder	1 tsp
Red chilli powder	½ tsp
Garam masala powder	½ tsp
Raw mango, peeled and chopped/lime juice	1 small mango or juice of 2 lemons

METHOD

Mix all the ingredients and grind to a paste.

Note: You can also add 2-3 pods of garlic.

Coconut Chutney

INGREDIENTS

Coconut	½
Green chillies	2–3
Curry leaves	few
Salt	to taste
Mustard seeds	1 tsp
Oil	1 tbsp
Whole red chillies	2-3
Tamarind juice	½ cup
Or	
Lime juice	4 tbsp

METHOD

1. Grind coconut, green chillies, salt and coriander leaves in a grinder.
2. Mix tamarind juice in it.

TO SEASON

1. Heat oil and fry mustard seeds. When they start to crackle, add curry leaves and whole red chillies.
2. Pour this on the chutney and serve.

Onion and Tomato Chutney

INGREDIENTS

Onion	1
Tomatoes	2
Red chilli powder	1 tsp
Salt	to taste
Mustard seed	½ tsp
Curry leaves	few
Lime Juice	2 tbsp
Sugar	1 tsp

METHOD

1. Grind onion and tomatoes to a paste.
2. Heat oil in a pan and add mustard seeds, curry leaves and after 2 minutes add the onion-tomato paste. Fry till paste becomes thick.
3. Add salt, red chilli powder and lime juice.
4. Serve cold.

Boiled Rice

Use long-grain rice for the recipes in this book. Basmati rice gives a better flavour in cooking and old Basmati rice is preferred for a good texture.

FOR PULAO

Rice	1 cup
Water	4 ½ cups

METHOD

1. Wash the rice thoroughly under running water, then place it in a bowl. Soak in water for 30 minutes. Drain.
2. Bring the measured water to a boil, add the rice and bring back to a boil again. Reduce heat and simmer for 15–20 minutes. Take care to see rice is not overcooked and that the grains remain separate. The rice should not become soggy.
3. Drain the rice and allow to cool before use.

Note: Add juice of half lemon while cooking to make fluffy rice. You can also add star aniseed while boiling to lend the rice rich aroma.

BOILED DAL

INGREDIENTS

Dal	1 cup
Water	2 cups

METHOD

1. Wash the *dal* under plenty of cold running water.
2. In a saucepan, boil the *dal* with the given amount of water. Reduce heat and cover the pan. Simmer until water is absorbed and the dal is tender—the cooking time varies depending on the type of *dal*.

TOMATO PUREE

INGREDIENTS

Ripe tomatoes	1 kg
Water	4 cups

METHOD

1. Wash and boil the tomatoes with water for 10 minutes.
2. Remove the skins and churn in the mixer. Store in an airtight container and keep in the freezer. Use for cooking whenever required.

WHITE SAUCE

INGREDIENTS

Butter	3 tbsp
Cornflour	3 tbsp
Milk	2 cups

METHOD

1. Heat a pan, add butter and cornflour. On slow fire, keep stirring till cornflour stops sticking to the pan (i.e. for 2–3 minutes).
2. Remove the pan from the fire and add cold milk. Keep stirring.
3. Put the pan back on the fire and stir till the mixture boils and the sauce thickens.
4. Cool and use for cooking. This sauce cannot be stored.

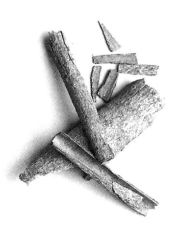

GARAM MASALA

INGREDIENTS

Black cardamoms	8-10
Green cardamoms	15–20
Cinnamons (1 inch each)	15–20
Cloves	1 tbsp
Mace	1 flower
Nutmeg	1
Peppercorns	1 tbsp
Cumin seeds	½ cup
Coriander seeds	2 tbsp

METHOD

1. Lightly roast the above ingredients and then grind to a fine powder. Store in an air-tight container and use when required.

KASHMIRI GARAM MASALA

INGREDIENTS

Green cardamom	4 tsp
Black cumin seeds	2 tsp
Peppercorns	2 tsp
Cinnamon sticks (1")	6
Cloves	1 tsp
Grated nutmeg	½ tsp

METHOD

1. Lightly roast the above ingredients and then grind to a fine powder. Store in an air-tight container and use when required.

RASAM POWDER

INGREDIENTS

Coriander powder	2 cups
Peppercorns	¼ cup
Cumin seeds	¼ cup
Fenugreek seeds	4 tsp
Curry leaves	1 bunch
Red chillies, chopped	2 cups
Turmeric powder	1 tsp
Oil	2 tsp

METHOD

1. Fry the red chillies in oil.
2. Dry-roast the rest of the ingredients. Add fried red chillies.
3. Grind finely and store in an airtight container.

SAMBHAR POWDER

INGREDIENTS

Coriander seeds	2 cups
Cumin seeds	¼ cup
Fenugreek seeds	2 tsp
Red chillies, chopped	2 cups
Turmeric powder	2 tsp
Mustard seeds	2 tsp
Poppy seeds	2 tsp
Bengal gram (*chana dal*)	½ cup
Oil	2 tsp

METHOD

1. Roast all the ingredients.
2. Grind finely and store in an airtight container.

Note: Rasam *and* sambhar *powders, paneer, ghee, khoya, tomato puree and even curd are readily available in the market.*

Regional Menus

1. Gujarati

2. Rajasthani

3. Punjabi

4. Karnataka

5. Andhra

6. Kerala

7. Tamil

8. Maharashtrian

9. Kashmiri

10. Bengali

11. Goan

12. Mughlai

13. Uttar Pradesh

1 GUJARATI MENU

Chaach
Gujarati Kadhi
Khatti Mithi Dal
Makai Ni Khichdi
Vaingan Vatana Nu Shak
Methi Thepla
Kesari Shrikhand

CHAACH

(Flavoured buttermilk)

INGREDIENTS

Fresh curd	2 cups
Black salt	½ tsp
Sugar	1 tsp
Salt	to taste
Roasted cumin seed powder	1 tsp
Green chilli-ginger paste	½ tsp
Fresh coriander leaves, finely chopped	1 tbsp

METHOD

1. Beat the curd till smooth.
2. Mix all ingredients including curd with 4 cups of water; add 5-6 ice cubes and churn well in a mixer. Serve chilled.

GUJARATI KADHI

(Gramflour curry flavoured with jaggery)

INGREDIENTS

Curd	2 cups
Water	2 cups
Gramflour	1½ tbsp
Green chilli-ginger paste	1 tsp
Jaggery, powdered	1 tbsp
Turmeric powder	¼ tsp
Salt	to taste
Clarified butter/Refined oil	1 tbsp
Cumin seeds	1 tsp
Cinnamon	1-2
Cloves	4-6
Curry leaves	7-8
Coriander leaves, chopped	1 tbsp

METHOD

1. Mix the curd with gramflour and beat till smooth. Add water, chilli-ginger paste, turmeric powder, salt and mix well.
2. Heat oil in a pan and add cumin seeds. As the seeds turn golden brown, add cloves and cinnamon. Now add the curry leaves and pour the curd mixture. Keep stirring till it boils. Cook for 10-15 minutes.
3. Add jaggery and bring to a boil once more. Garnish with coriander leaves.
4. Serve hot with plain rice.

KHATTI MITHI DAL

(Sweet and sour lentil)

INGREDIENTS

Split red gram (*arhar/toor dal*)	1 cup
Green chilli-ginger paste	2 tsp
Turmeric powder	½ tsp
Coriander powder	1 tsp
Curry leaves	6-7
Green peas	2 tbsp
Red chilli powder	½ tsp
Salt	to taste
Jaggery, powdered	1 tbsp
Tamarind juice	¼ cup
Oil	1 tbsp
Mustard seeds	½ tsp
Whole red chillies	2
Asafoetida (*hing*)	a pinch
Coconut, grated	1 tbsp
Coriander leaves	a few

METHOD

1. Wash the *dal* and pressure-cook with 2 cups of water, salt and turmeric powder. After the first whistle, cook on slow fire for 10 minutes. Remove from fire and mash thoroughly.

2. Add 3 cups of water, chilli-ginger paste, red chilli powder, coriander powder, green peas and curry leaves.

3. Bring *dal* to boil and add jaggery and tamarind juice. Cook for 5 minutes.

4. To temper the *dal,* heat 1 tbsp of oil separately, ½ tsp of mustard seeds, a pinch of asafoetida and red chillies. Wait for the mustard seeds to crackle and add to the hot *dal.*

5. Garnish with grated coconut and chopped coriander leaves and serve hot.

MAKAI NI KHICHDI

(Corn gruel)

INGREDIENTS

Whole corn pieces (*bhutta*), peeled and grated	4
Green gram (*moong dal*)	½ cup
Sugar	1 tsp
Salt	to taste
Lemon	½
Coriander leaves, chopped	2 tbsp
Rice	1 cup

FOR THE *TADKA* (SEASONING)

Oil	2 tbsp
Mustard seeds	1 tsp
Cumin seeds	1 tsp
Asafoetida (*hing*)	a pinch
Green chillies, chopped	2

METHOD

1. Wash the *dal.* Soak the rice for 10-15 minutes.

2. Heat oil, add mustard and cumin seeds, asafoetida and green chillies and fry till the seeds start to crackle.

3. Add corn and cook on slow flame for 5 minutes. Add salt and sugar.

4. Add enough water and *dal* and rice. Cover and cook till the *khichdi* is soft (add some boiling water if *khichdi* looks thick).

5. Add lemon juice to taste and mix well. Garnish with coriander leaves and serve hot.

VAINGAN VATANA NU SHAK

(Brinjal and green peas in spicy masala)

INGREDIENTS

Brinjal (round and big)	1, approx 300 gms
Green peas, shelled	1 cup
Turmeric powder	½ tsp
Coriander powder	2 tsp
Cumin seed powder	½ tsp
Chilli powder	½ tsp
Salt	to taste
Oil	3 tbsp
Asafoetida (*hing*)	a pinch
Green chilli paste	½ tsp
Coriander leaves, chopped	1 tbsp
Garlic cloves	4-5
Ginger	½" piece

METHOD

1. Wash and dice the brinjal into 1" cubes.

2. Grind coriander (3 tbsp), ginger, garlic and chilli into a paste.

3. Heat oil in a wok (*kadhai*) and add asafoetida. Now add cut brinjal pieces, shelled peas and the above paste; sauté for a minute.

4. Add all the other ingredients and mix well.

5. Add ½ cup water, cover and cook on slow fire for 15-20 minutes.

6. Garnish with one tbsp of chopped coriander leaves and serve hot.

METHI THEPLA

(Wheatflour bread flavoured with fenugreek leaves)

INGREDIENTS

Wheatflour (*atta*)	1 cup
Curd	¼ cup
Oil	1 tbsp
Fresh fenugreek leaves (*methi*), chopped	½ cup
Turmeric powder	¼ tsp
Chilli powder	½ tsp
Salt	1 tsp
Sugar	½ tsp

METHOD

1. Mix all the ingredients with wheatflour. Add ¼ cup water to make a soft dough. Keep aside for 15-20 minutes.

2. Divide the dough into 8-9 equal portions. With a rolling pin, roll out each portion very thinly to get a 6"-diameter *roti*. Cook on a hot griddle (*tava*) using a little oil.

3. Serve either hot or cold.

KESARI SHRIKHAND

(Saffron-flavoured chilled yogurt, garnished with dry fruits)

INGREDIENTS

Thick and fresh curd made from full-cream milk	4 cups
Sugar, powdered	1 cup
Saffron (*kesar*), soaked in 1 tbsp warm milk	¼ tsp
Cardamom powder	½ tsp
Nutmeg powder	¼ tsp
Cream	2 tbsp
Almonds, ground to pieces	4-5
Pistachios, ground to pieces	4-5

METHOD

1. Tie the freshly set curd in a muslin cloth and let it hang for 3-4 hrs.
2. Pass this curd through a sieve or strainer to make it smooth.
3. Add powdered sugar, cardamom, nutmeg powder, saffron, cream and mix well.
4. Pour into a serving dish, garnish with almonds and pistachios; refrigerate for 1 hour.
5. Serve chilled.

RAJASTHANI MENU

Rajasthani Dal
Batti
Chokha
Baingan Bhurta
Churma
Gatte Ki Sabji
Rabri

RAJASTHANI DAL

(Mixed pulses)

INGREDIENTS

Washed green gram (*moong dal*)	
Bengal gram (*chana dal*)	
Split red gram (*arhar dal*)	
Washed lentil (*masoor dal*)	¼ cup each
Salt	to taste
Turmeric	½ tsp
Bay leaves	2
Asafoetida (*hing*)	a pinch
Dry mango powder (*amchur*)	1 tsp
Red Chilli powder	½ tsp
Oil	2 tbsp
Cumin seeds	½ tsp
Red chilli pickle stuffed with black masala (readily available)	2-3 whole red chillies

METHOD

1. Wash and mix the *dals* in one pan. Pressure-cook with salt, turmeric powder, bay leaves and 3 cups of water.
2. Mix red chilli pickle into the dal and add *amchur*.
3. In a separate pan, heat oil. Fry asafoetida, cumin seeds and red chilli powder.

4. Now add this to the *dal* such that this *tadka* (seasoning) floats on top. Serve hot.

BATTI

(Small stuffed wheatflour pancakes)

INGREDIENTS

FOR DOUGH

Wheatflour (*atta*)	2 cups
Salt	to taste
Carom seeds (*ajwain*)	½ tsp
Oil	1 tbsp

FOR FILLING

OPTION 1:

Roasted chickpeas (*chana*), powdered	½ cup
Onion, chopped	1
Salt	to taste
Ground red chillies	½ tsp
Dry mango (*amchur*) powder	½ tsp
Red chilli pickle	1 tbsp

OPTION 2:

Peas, boiled	½ cup
Potatoes, boiled and mashed	2
Salt	to taste
Red chilli powder	½ tsp
Green chillies, chopped	2
Dry mango (*amchur*) powder	½ tsp
Garam masala powder	½ tsp
Clarified butter (*ghee*)	for frying
Red chilli pickle	1 tbsp

METHOD

1. Mix all the ingredients for the filling and keep aside.
2. Mix all the ingredients for the dough

using some water. Keep aside for 10-15 minutes.

3. Divide the dough in small portions. Flatten each portion on your palm, stuff with the filling and close nicely from all sides.

4. Roast these *batties* in a hot gas *tandoor* (oven) till they become golden brown from all sides.

5. Heat clarified butter in a pan, press the *batties* with your hand and fry for 2-3 minutes. Serve immediately with steaming *dal*.

CHOKHA

(Mashed potatoes flavoured with red chilli and dry mango powder)

INGREDIENTS

Potatoes, boiled, peeled and mashed	4
Onions, sliced	2
Salt	to taste
Garam masala powder	½ tsp
Red chilli powder	½ tsp
Dry mango powder (*amchur*)	¾ tsp
Green chillies	1 chopped
Whole red pickled chillies	2
Coriander leaves, chopped	a few sprigs

METHOD

1. Mix all the ingredients, except green chillies and coriander leaves.

2. Garnish with green chillies and coriander leaves and serve.

BAINGAN BHURTA

(Spicy roasted mashed brinjal)

INGREDIENTS

Brinjal (round)	1 medium (200 gm)
Onion	1 big
Ginger	1 small
Green chilli	1
Tomato	2 medium
Coriander leaves	few
Salt	to taste
Red chilli powder	1 tsp
Garam masala powder	to taste
Clarified butter (*ghee*)	1 tsp

METHOD

1. Roast the brinjal on open fire by smearing its outsides with oil.

2. Remove its peel and mash the insides.

3. Chop onion, ginger, green chilli and fry lightly in hot clarified butter.

4. Add tomato pulp, salt, red chilli powder, *garam masala* and mashed brinjal. Mix well and continue to fry till the mixture blends and oil separates.

5. Serve garnished with chopped coriander leaves and *garam masala* powder.

Churma

(Wheatflour dessert)

INGREDIENTS

Wheatflour (*atta*)	2 cups
Castor sugar	1 cup
Clarified butter (*ghee*)	½ cup
Water	as required for dough

METHOD

1. Add ¾ cup water to wheatflour and knead as when making dough for *chapatis*. Keep aside for 10-15 minutes.
2. Roll out a portion of the dough, apply clarified butter and close it. Then spread it out again to make a thick *parantha*-like shape.
3. Cook on a hot griddle (*tava*) by applying *ghee* to both sides of the *parantha*.
4. Repeat the above steps for the rest of the dough.
5. Mash the *paranthas*, break into small pieces and crush well. Add castor sugar to this.
6. Heat *ghee* in a pan. Toss the crushed pieces in it and serve hot.

Gatte Ki Sabji

(Gramflour balls' curry)

INGREDIENTS
FOR GATTE

Gramflour (besan)	1 cup
Dry fenugreek leaves (*kasoori methi*)	1 tbsp
Salt	to taste
Red chilli powder	1 tsp
Garam masala powder	1 tsp

FOR CURRY

Plain curd (preferably 2-3 days old)	3 cups
Salt	to taste
Turmeric powder	½ tsp
Kasoori methi	½ tsp
Red chilli powder	1 tsp
Oil	2 tbsp
Asafoetida (*hing*)	1 tbsp
Cumin seed powder	1 tsp
Garam masala powder	1 tsp

METHOD

1. Mix the ingredients for the *gatte*, add a little water and 1 tsp oil. Knead like dough.
2. In a pan, boil 4 cups of water.
3. Roll the dough into small elongated and cylindrical shapes (4-5 pieces) of about ½-inch thickness and 8-inch length.
4. Place these cylinders in boiling water for 10 minutes.
5. Remove extra water. Cut cylinders into ½-inch sizes. Keep them aside.
6. Beat curd with 1 tsp of *besan*.
7. Heat oil in a vessel, fry asafoetida and cumin seeds till the seeds turn golden brown. Add red chilli powder first and then beaten curd.

8. Add salt, turmeric powder, dry *methi* leaves. Keep stirring till the mixture boils.

9. Add the cylinders (*gatte*) to the curry. Cover and cook for 10-15 minutes.

10. Garnish with *garam masala* powder and serve hot.

RABRI

INGREDIENTS

Whole milk	6 cups
Saffron	few strands
Sugar	¼ cup
Green cardamom powder	½ tsp
Cashewnuts, chopped	4-6
Almonds, sliced	4-6
Pistachios	4-6

METHOD

1. Boil the milk with saffron in a thick bottomed or a non-stick vessel, stirring occasionally on medium heat. Cook for about 30 minutes till the milk reduces to half.

2. Add sugar and continue to simmer on low heat for 12-15 minutes till the milk becomes rich and thick.

3. Remove from fire and add cardamom powder, cashewnut pieces, sliced almonds and pistachios. Serve hot or cold, as desired.

3

PUNJABI MENU

Dal Tamatar Shorba
Chilli Cherry Tomato Salad
Punjabi Kadhi
Dahi Vada
Paneer Bhurji
Pindi Chole
Bhatoora
Gajar Halwa

DAL TAMATAR SHORBA

(*Lentil and tomato soup*)

INGREDIENTS

Onions, sliced	2
Garlic, crushed	2 cloves
Washed lentils (*masoor dal*)	1 cup
Red chilli powder	¼ tsp
Tomatoes, chopped	1 kg
Oil	1 tbsp
Salt	to taste
Cooked rice	2 tbsp
Lime juice	1 tbsp
Coriander leaves (chopped)	1 tbsp

METHOD

1. Heat oil in a pan. Add onions and garlic and fry for 2 minutes. Add the *dal* and tomatoes, continue to cook for 5-7 minutes.
2. Pour 4 cups of water and bring to a boil. Reduce the heat. Cover the pan and simmer until *dal* is soft.
3. Allow the soup to cool slightly, blend in a liquidiser and strain through a sieve.
4. Boil soup, add rice, salt and chilli powder.
5. Garnish with chopped coriander leaves and serve hot.

CHILLI CHERRY TOMATO SALAD

INGREDIENTS

Cherry tomatoes	250 gm
Potatoes, boiled, peeled and cut into cubes	1 cup
Onion, cut into cubes	1 large
Cucumber, cut into cubes	1
Fresh whole red chillies, slit into half	3-4
Salt	to taste
Roasted sesame seeds (*til*)	2 tbsp
Vinegar	4 tbsp
Salad leaves	a few
Sugar	1 tsp

METHOD

1. Soak red chillies in vinegar for 1 hour. Add salt and sugar to the vinegar.
2. Toss all the vegetables in this.
3. Serve on a bed of lettuce, garnish with roasted sesame seeds.

Punjabi Kadhi

(Gramflour balls in spicy tangy curry)

INGREDIENTS

FOR CURRY:

Curd	2 cups
Gramflour (*besan*)	2 tbsp
Salt	to taste
Turmeric powder	½ tsp
Fenugreek seeds	1 tsp
Carom seeds	½ tsp
Mustard seeds	½ tsp
Cumin seeds (*jeera*)	½ tsp
Bay leaves	2
Dry fenugreek leaves (*kasoori methi*)	1 tbsp

FOR GRAMFLOUR BALLS (VADAS):

Gram Flour	4 tbsp
Salt	to taste
Red chilli powder	½ tsp
Garam masala powder	½ tbsp
Onion, chopped	1
Green chillies chopped	1
Soda bicarbonate	a pinch
Oil	for deep frying

FOR TEMPERING (TADKA):

Oil	2 tbsp
Whole red chillies	4-5
Red chilli powder	1 tsp

METHOD

1. Beat the curd with gramflour. Take care to see that there aren't any lumps formed.
2. Heat oil, add cumin, fenugreek, carom and mustard seeds. When they begin to crackle, add curry leaves and beaten curd.
3. Add 4 cups of water, stirring continuously till it boils.
4. Add salt, *kasoori methi* and turmeric powder, mix well and leave on slow fire for ½ an hour. Your *kadhi* is ready.
5. Mix the ingredients for *vada* using enough water. Leave the mixture aside for 10 minutes.
6. Make *vadas* (small balls) of walnut-size from the mixture. Heat oil and fry the *vadas* on slow fire till golden brown.
7. Soak them in 4 cups of water for 10 minutes.
8. Squeeze excess water from *vadas* and immerse them in *kadhi*. Bring *kadhi* to a boil and cook for 5 minutes.
9. Pour into a serving dish.
10. Heat oil for *tadka;* fry whole red chillies and chilli powder for 1 minute. Pour on the *kadhi* and serve hot.

Dahi Vada

(Gramflour balls in tangy yogurt with chutneys)

INGREDIENTS

Washed green gram (*moong dal*)	1 cup
Salt	to taste
Red chilli powder	½ tsp
Cumin seed (*jeera*) powder	¼ tsp
Soda bi-carbonate	a pinch
Oil	for deep-frying

FOR GARNISHING:

Beaten Curd	1 cup
Tamarind chutney	4 tbsp
Mint chutney	2 tbsp
Salt, red chilli and roasted cumin seed powders	to taste
Chaat masala powder	1 tsp

1. Soak the *dal* overnight in water. Drain and grind to a paste without adding any more water.

2. Add salt, red chilli powder, cumin seeds and soda bi-carbonate to the above mixture.

3. Beat nicely till smooth and fluffy.

4. Heat oil in a pan on slow fire.

5. With the mixture, make balls slightly bigger than bite-sized and fry till light brown.

6. Soak balls in salt-water for 10 to 15 minutes.

7. Squeeze out excess water and immerse them in beaten curd.

8. Transfer to a serving dish, garnish with mint and tamarind chutneys and all the spices.

9. Chill and serve.

PANEER BHURJI

(Dry savoury cottage cheese)

INGREDIENTS

Cottage cheese (*paneer*), grated	2 cups
Peas, boiled	½ cup
Onion, chopped	1 cup
Tomatoes, chopped	2 cups
Salt	to taste
Capsicum, chopped	¾ cup
Cumin seeds (whole)	1 tsp
Cumin seed powder	1 tsp
Turmeric powder	½ tsp
Coriander powder	1½ tsp
Red chilli powder	1 tsp

Oil	3 tbsp
Cream	2 tbsp
White butter	1 tbsp
Dry mango (*amchur*) powder	1 tsp

METHOD

1. Heat oil in a pan and add cumin seeds. When they turn brown, add onion slices and fry till they become golden brown.

2. Add tomatoes and fry till they are soft. Add all the spices except *amchur*. Fry for 5-6 minutes.

3. Add *paneer*, peas and capsicum and mix well. Add ¼ cup of water. Cover and cook till capsicum is soft.

4. Add cream and butter and sprinkle *amchur* powder. Mix well and serve hot.

PINDI CHOLE

(Spicy white chickpeas)

INGREDIENTS

White chickpeas (*chana/chhole*)	1cup
Onions	2
Potatoes	1
Ginger, cut lengthwise	1/4th cup
Salt	to taste
Black pepper	1 tsp
Roasted cumin seed powder	1 tsp
Dry mango powder (*amchur*)	¾ tsp
Green chillies, chopped	2
Lime juice	3 tbsp
Coriander leaves, chopped	a few
Tea liquor	3 cups
Garam masala powder	¾ tsp
Oil	3-4 tbsp

METHOD

1. Soak the *chana* overnight in water.
2. Pressure-cook the *chana* with salt and tea liquor.
3. Cut potatoes in big sizes and deep fry till golden brown.
4. Cut onions in big sizes.
5. Heat oil in a pan, add *chana*, potatoes, onions, ginger, black pepper, green chillies, roasted cumin seed, dry mango and *garam masala* powders. Cook for 5 to 10 minutes. Mix well with lime juice.
6. Garnish with coriander leaves and serve.

Note: For tea liquor: Boil 4-5 tsp tea leaves in 4 cups of water. Strain and store the liquor.

BHATOORA

(Fluffy flour bread)

INGREDIENTS

Flour (*maida*)	1 cup
Oil	for deep-frying and kneading
Salt	to taste
Soda powder	½ tsp
Curd	3 tbsp

METHOD

1. Knead the flour with a little oil, salt, curd and soda powder.
2. Keep aside for half-an-hour.
3. Divide the dough in four parts. Out of each portion, make a ball and flatten out with rolling pin into 5-6" oval-shaped pieces (*bhatooras*).

4. Deep-fry the *bhatooras* till they turn golden brown.
5. Serve with spicy black *chana*.

GAJAR HALWA

(Carrot pudding)

INGREDIENTS

Carrot	1 kg
Milk	4 cups
Sugar	¾ cup
Almonds, soaked, peeled and chopped	2 tbsp

METHOD

1. Wash, peel and grate the carrots.
2. In a heated wok, dry roast the grated carrot for 5 minutes.
3. And boiled milk and keep on slow fire for 1-2 hours.
4. Keep stirring.
5. When the milk has totally dried up, add sugar and stir for 10 minutes.
6. Garnish with almonds and serve hot.

KARNATAKA MENU

Tomato Rasam
Kosumbari
Sambhar
Ghopikai Uppakari
Bisi Bele Bhath
Chitraana
Raagi Roti
Sevian Payasam

TOMATO RASAM

(Tangy tomato soup)

INGREDIENTS

Tomatoes, chopped	4, medium-sized
Tamarind juice	1 tbsp
Curry leaves	a few
Garlic, chopped	1 tbsp
Whole red chillies, roughly broken	3-4
Mustard seeds	½ tsp
Coriander leaves, chopped	a few
Salt	to taste
Oil	2 tbsp
Rasam powder	1 tbsp

METHOD

1. Boil tomatoes and tamarind with 4 cups of water.
2. Strain the mixture and keep aside.
3. Heat oil in a pan, add mustard seeds. When they start to crackle, add curry leaves, whole red chillies, chopped garlic and *rasam* powder. After 2 minutes, add the strained mixture.
4. Add salt and boil. Cook for 4-5 minutes.
5. Garnish with coriander leaves and serve hot with plain rice.

KOSUMBARI

(Green gram salad)

INGREDIENTS

Washed green gram (*moong dal*)	½ cup
Salt	to taste
Green chillies, chopped	2
Fresh coconut, grated	3 tbsp
Coriander leaves, chopped	few
Lime juice	2 tbsp

METHOD

1. Wash the *dal* and soak in water for 2 hours.
2. Remove extra water from *dal*, mix all the ingredients and serve.

SAMBHAR

(Mixed vegetables in pulses curry and spicy masala)

INGREDIENTS

Split red gram (*arhar dal*)	½ cup
Whole red chillies	2-3
Turmeric powder	½ tsp
Mustard seeds	1 tsp
Tamarind juice	½ cup
Drumsticks, cut into long pieces	2
Onions, sliced	2 medium sized
Tomatoes	2
Potato, boiled and cut into cubes	1
Brinjals, cut into four pieces	2 small sized
Carrot, peeled and cut into cubes	1
Curry leaves	a few
Oil	2 tbsp
Sambhar powder	2-3 tsp
Asafoetida (*hing*)	a pinch

METHOD

1. Wash the *dal*, add 4 cups of water, salt and turmeric powder and pressure-cook.
2. Heat oil in a pan, fry onions till soft.
3. Add all the vegetables, including the drumsticks, to the onions and cover and cook for a few minutes till they are soft.
4. Add tamarind juice. Bring to a boil and cook for 5 minutes. Then add the cooked *dal*.
5. Heat oil in a separate pan, add mustard seeds. Wait till they crackle and add curry leaves and whole red chillies. Pour this over the *sambhar*.
6. Add *sambhar* powder and *hing* after half-a-minute.
7. Boil and simmer for 5 minutes and serve hot.

METHOD FOR TAMARIND JUICE

1. Soak 1 tbsp of tamarind in ½ cup of water for ½ an hour.
2. Mash nicely with hand and strain the juice.

GHOPIKAI UPPAKARI

(Cluster beans with coconut)

INGREDIENTS

Cluster beans	500 gms/5 cups when sliced
Oil	3 tbsp
Mustard seeds	1 tbsp
Bengal gram (*chana dal*)	1 tsp
Whole red chillies	3-4
Curry leaves	a few
Asafoetida (*hing*)	a pinch
Green chillies, chopped	2-3
Coconut, grated	4 tbsp
Salt	to taste

METHOD

1. Cut the beans into fine slices. Blanch and set aside.
2. Heat oil and add mustard seeds. When they start to crackle, add *dal*.
3. When the *dal* turns golden, add curry leaves, red chillies, asafoetida, green chillies and sauté for 1 minute. Add beans and salt.
4. Sprinkle a little water, cover and cook on slow fire.
5. When beans are done, add grated coconut and stir for 2 minutes. Serve hot.

Bisi Bele Bhath

(Mixed vegetables and rice)

INGREDIENTS
RICE:

Rice	1 cup
Split red gram (*toor dal*)	1 cup
Tamarind (soaked in water)	1 small ball
Grated coconut	½ cup

VEGETABLES:

Carrots cut into bite-sized pieces	1
Beans, cut into medium-sized pieces	10
Sliced cabbage	¼ cup
Peas	¼ cup
Potatoes, cut medium-sized	2 small
Tomatoes	2

SPICES:

Coriander seeds	4 tbsp
Dry red chillies	10
Bengal gram (*chana dal*)	2 tbsp
Black gram (*urad dal*)	1 tbsp
Cinnamon sticks	2
Cloves	3-4

FOR SEASONING:

Asafoetida (*hing*)	a pinch
Mustard seeds	1 tsp
Curry leaves	a few

FOR GARNISH:

Raw groundnuts	½ cup
Khara or spicy *boondi* (available in the market)	2 tbsp

METHOD

1. Boil the rice and keep aside.
2. Boil the *toor dal* along with all the vegetables in a pressure cooker till *dal* is cooked. Keep aside.
3. Heat 1 tsp of oil in a wok and fry the spice on slow fire. When cool, grind to a paste with grated coconut.
4. Mix the dal-vegetables-*masala* mixture with a spoon, taking care not to mash the vegetables.
5. Keep the mixture on fire and bring to a boil. Turn the flame to low and add tamarind juice. Allow to cook for sometime.
6. You could, at this stage, pour 2 tsp of *ghee* on the *dal* mixture. But this is optional.
7. Fry asafoetida, mustard seeds and curry leaves slightly and pour on the *dal* mixture. Bring to a boil and cook for only a minute.
8. Add the boiled rice and allow to further boil and cook for 2-3 minutes.
9. Serve with groundnuts and *khara boondi* sprinkled on top.

CHITRAANA

(Lemon rice)

INGREDIENTS

Cooked rice	2 cups
Lemon juice	5 tbsp
Salt	to taste
Oil	2 tbsp
Mustard seeds	½ tsp
Bengal gram (*chana dal*)	1 tsp
Curry leaves	a few
Green chillies, chopped	3-4
Turmeric powder	¼ tsp
Cashewnuts	5-6
Roasted peanuts	2 tbsp
Washed urad dal	1 tsp

METHOD

1. Mix the lemon juice, salt and cooked rice and keep aside.
2. Heat oil; add mustard seeds. Wait till they crackle and add the *chana & urad dal*. Stir until golden brown. Add curry leaves.
3. Add the rest of the ingredients and cook for 3 minutes.
4. Add the rice and cook on slow fire for another 5 minutes.
5. Garnish with cashewnuts and serve hot.

RAAGI ROTI

(Stuffed raagi flour bread)

INGREDIENTS

FOR ROTI:

Raagi flour	1 cup
Water	2 cups
Salt	1 tsp

FOR FILLING:

Cumin seeds	½ tsp
Asafoetida (*hing*)	a pinch
Onions, chopped	2
Green chillies, chopped	2
Coconut, grated	2 tbsp
Oil	4 tsp
Coriander leaves, chopped	2 tbsp

METHOD

1. Boil water with salt in it. Mix *raagi* flour with this water, taking care not to form lumps. Keep stirring on slow fire.
2. Remove from fire and cool.
3. Add some more *raagi* flour to the above mixture and form a dough.
4. Heat oil in a pan. Add asafoetida and cumin seeds. Fry for a minute and add onions and green chillies. Fry till onions become golden brown.
5. Add coconut and coriander leaves and a little salt. Remove from fire.
6. Divide the dough into 5-6 circular discs.
7. Roll out the discs into flat shapes and fill with the onion filling you have just made. Close the discs into balls tightly, taking care to ensure there aren't any cracks.
8. Roll out again gently.
9. Roast *rotis* on a hot griddle. Apply oil on both sides and cook till golden brown.
10. Serve hot with vegetables.

SEVIAN PAYASAM

(Vermicelli pudding)

INGREDIENTS

Milk	**4 cups**
Brown vermicelli	**½ cup**
Sugar	**½ cup**
Cardamom syrup/	**a few drops**
crushed cardamom	**½ tsp**
Chopped nuts	**2 tbsp**
Saffron (*kesar*), soaked in 1 tbsp milk	**2-3 leaves**
Clarified butter (*ghee*)	**1 tbsp**

METHOD

1. Heat *ghee* in a wok. Break the vermicelli into it and fry for sometime.
2. Add milk and keep stirring till it boils.
3. Add *kesar* and cardamom syrup and let it simmer for 15-20 minutes.
4. Add sugar while stirring the mixture constantly.
5. Garnish with nuts and serve hot.

ANDHRA MENU

Ullpaya Sambhar
Mirchi Ka Salan
Bangala Dumpa Vepudu
Kurmu Pulusu
Chintakaya Puliohara
Sweet Potato Kheer

ULLPAYA SAMBHAR

(Spicy pulses curry with small onions)

INGREDIENTS

Split red gram (*toor dal*)	**1 cup**
Turmeric powder	**½ tsp**
Asafoetida (*hing*)	**a pinch**
Garlic	**6 cloves**
Tamarind	**1 small ball**
Oil	**2 tbsp**
Clarified butter/*Ghee*	**1 tsp**
Cumin seeds	**¼ tsp**
Mustard seeds	**¼ tsp**
Black gram (*urad dal*)	**¼ tsp**
Curry leaves	**6**
Small onions	**250 gm/2½ cups**
Green chillies, chopped	**2**
Tomatoes, chopped	**2**
Sambhar powder	**4 tsp**
Salt	**to taste**
Red chilli powder	**1 tsp**
Coriander leaves, chopped	**a few**

METHOD

1. Soak the *toor dal* for half-an-hour.
   Pressure-cook till soft in 4 cups of water
   with salt, turmeric powder, asafoetida and
   2 cloves of garlic.

2. Soak tamarind in ½ cup of water for 20
   minutes, squeeze well and strain out the
   pulp. Keep aside.

3. Heat oil in a pan, fry cumin seeds,
   mustard seeds, *urad dal* and curry leaves
   till they turn brown.

4. Add onions, green chillies and rest of the
   garlic.

5. When onions become soft, add tomatoes
   and fry on low flame for 5 minutes. Add
   red chilli powder.

6. Add this to the cooked *dal* along with
   sambhar powder and tamarind pulp.
   Simmer till the mixture has a rich aroma.
   Add *ghee*.

7. Add chopped coriander leaves and serve
   hot with boiled rice.

MIRCHI KA SALAN

(Green chilli curry)

INGREDIENTS

Green chillies, (long and thick)	250 gm
Salt	to taste
Oil	¼ cup
Onions, finely sliced	6
Ginger paste	2 tsp
Turmeric powder	½ tsp
Coriander powder	1 tbsp
Coconut, ground and dry	1 tbsp
Sesame seeds, grounded	1 tbsp
Cumin seeds	1 tbsp
Roasted cumin seed powder	1 tbsp
Curry leaves	few
Tamarind juice	1½ cup
Coriander leaves, chopped	few
Mint leaves	few

METHOD

1. Slit chillies lengthwise, soak them in salt-water for half-an-hour and drain. Heat oil and fry chillies till they begin to change colour and brown slightly. Remove from oil and keep aside.

2. In the same oil, add cumin seeds and fry onions till they become brown. Add ginger and garlic and fry for a few minutes.

3. Add turmeric powder, coriander powder, coconut, sesame seeds, cumin seed powder and curry leaves and continue to fry on slow heat.

4. Add the chillies, mix well and cook. Add tamarind juice. Boil on slow flame till water dries up a little.

5. Garnish with coriander and mint leaves and serve hot.

BANGALA DUMPA VEPUDU

(Spicy potato curry)

INGREDIENTS

Potatoes, boiled and cut into small pieces	4
Tomatoes, boiled, peeled and chopped	4
Mustard seeds	½ tsp
Black gram (*urad dal*), washed	2 tsp
Bengal gram (*chana dal*)	2 tsp
Oil	¼ cup
Curry leaves	few
Red chilli powder	1½ tsp
Salt	to taste
Garlic, chopped	1 tbsp
Onion, finely chopped	1

METHOD

1. Heat oil in a wok, add mustard seeds, *urad dal* and *chana dal*. Fry till golden brown.

2. Add curry leaves, garlic and onion and again fry till onions are golden brown.

3. Add chopped tomatoes. Fry for sometime, add salt, red chilli powder and potatoes and mix well. Cover and cook on low flame for 2 minutes.

4. Serve hot.

KURMU PULUSU

(Raw jackfruit curry)

INGREDIENTS

Raw jackfruit, peeled and cut into 1½" pieces	1 kg/2 cups of cut pieces
Oil	¾ cup
Cardamoms	3
Cloves	3
Cinnamon stick	1" piece
Onions, finely sliced	4
Ginger paste	1 tsp
Garlic paste	1 tsp
Poppy seed paste	1 tsp
Coconut paste	1 tsp
Red chilli powder	1 tsp
Coriander powder	1 tbsp
Salt	to taste
Curd	1 cup
Bay leaves	2
Coriander leaves, chopped	few
Water	2 cups

METHOD

1. Heat oil and fry cardamoms, cloves and cinnamon till they crackle. Add jackfruit and fry till brown. Remove from oil and keep aside.
2. To the remaining oil, add chopped onions, ginger and garlic and fry.
3. Add all the spices and the bay leaves and fry well. Add the jackfruit and fry again. Now add beaten curd and water. Keep stirring till it boils.
4. Keep on slow fire till jackfruit is cooked.
5. Garnish with coriander leaves and serve hot.

CHINTAKAYA PULIOHARA

(Tamarind Rice)

INGREDIENTS

Rice, cooked	2 cups
Tamarind	50 gm/¼ cup
Oil	½ cup
Groundnuts	2 tbsp
Cumin seeds	1 tsp
Coriander seeds	1 tbsp
Dry red chillies	5
Fenugreek seeds	2 tbsp
Bengal gram (*chana dal*)	2 tbsp
Coconut, grated	½
Jaggery	1 tsp

FOR SEASONING:

Whole dry red chillies	4
Mustard seeds	1 tsp
Curry leaves	few
Asafoetida (*hing*)	a pinch
Turmeric powder	¼ tsp

METHOD

1. Soak tamarind in water for 20 minutes and extract the pulp.
2. Fry groundnuts, drain and keep aside.
3. Fry cumin seeds, coriander seeds, fenugreek seeds and dry red chillies. Grind them together.
4. Fry *chana dal* and boil in 1 cup of water until it softens.
5. Mix ground spices, *chana dal*, coconut, jaggery and tamarind pulp and cook together for a few minutes.
6. To season, heat oil in a pan and fry four red chillies, mustard seeds, curry leaves and asafoetida. Add rice, turmeric powder, and tamarind and spice mixture to the seasoning. Stir to mix.
7. Sprinkle groundnuts on rice and serve hot with plain curd.

SWEET POTATO KHEER

(Sweet potato pudding)

INGREDIENTS

Sweet potatoes	2 (large)
Milk	4 cups
Sugar	¾ cup
Cardamoms, powdered	4
Rose water	2 tsp
Raisins	1 tbsp
Oil	for deep-frying

FOR GARNISH:

Silver *varak*	(fine pieces of edible silver foil used for garnishing desserts)
Pistachios, finely sliced	6

METHOD

1. Peel and thinly grate the sweet potatoes. Deep-fry till golden grown.

2. Boil milk on low heat till it thickens.

3. Add cardamom powder, sugar and rose water.

4. Add raisins and fried potatoes and boil for 5 minutes.

5. Decorate with silver *varak* on top and sprinkle with chopped pistachios.

6. Serve hot or cold, as desired.

6 KERALA MENU

Pepper Rasam
Vegetable Stew
Appam
Avial
Alleppy Potato Curry
Paal Payasam

PEPPER RASAM

(Tangy pepper soup)

INGREDIENTS

Coriander leaves	¼ bunch
Cumin seeds	1 tsp
Coriander seeds	1 tsp
Garlic	4 cloves
Ginger	1 small piece
Tomatoes	2
Green chillies	1
Red chillies	2

Grind the above mixture to a paste and strain.

FOR RASAM:

Dal-water	2 cups
(water strained from cooked *toor* or yellow *moong dal*)	
Tamarind, soaked in water and pulp removed	1 lemon-sized ball
Salt	to taste
Turmeric powder	1 tsp
Pepper, crushed	2 tsp
Rasam powder	1 tsp (optional)

FOR SEASONING:

Clarified butter/Ghee	2 tsp
Cumin seeds	1 tsp
Curry leaves	1 sprig
Red chilli, slit into halves	1
Coriander leaves, chopped	a few
Mustard seeds	1 tsp

METHOD

1. Boil tamarind pulp, paste, salt and turmeric powder.

2. Add the ground spices' paste and *dal*-water. Bring to a boil and cook for 5-10 minutes.

3. Add pepper and rasam powder.

4. Heat *ghee*, add cumin and mustard seeds, and red chillies. Add curry leaves and season the *rasam* with this. Add chopped coriander leaves and serve hot.

VEGETABLE STEW

INGREDIENTS

Coconut	1
Carrots, potatoes, french beans and cauliflower florets, chopped and parboiled	2 cups
Onion, chopped	1
Cloves	2
Cinnamon sticks	2 small
Green chillies, chopped	1
Cornflour	1 tsp
Oil	1 tsp
Salt	to taste
Ginger, thinly sliced (optional)	a few slivers
Star aniseed	4-5

METHOD

1. Grate the coconut, add 2 cups of water and extract coconut milk after straining. Add cornflour, mix well and keep aside. (You can also use 2 cups of ready coconut milk instead.)

2. Heat oil in a griddle and fry the onion slices (and ginger slices if used) for 1 minute. Add cloves, star aniseed and cinnamon and fry again for a few seconds.

3. Add green chillies and salt and again fry for a few minutes. Add the coconut milk and vegetables and cook till vegetables are soft.

4. Remove from fire and serve hot.

APPAM

(Fluffy Kerala yeast bread)

INGREDIENTS

Raw rice	2 cups
Cooked rice	½ cup
Coconut	1
Sugar	2 tsp
Dry yeast	½ tsp
Salt	to taste
Oil	for cooking

METHOD

1. Wash the rice and soak for 2 to 3 hours and drain.

2. Grate the coconut, add 2 cups of water and extract coconut milk after straining.

3. Grind the raw rice and cooked rice together with a little coconut milk. Remove from grinder and add sugar, the remaining coconut milk and salt. Mix the yeast with a little warm water and add to the rice paste.

4. Mix well, ensuring the batter is of dropping consistency. Cover and keep for 2 to 3 hours.

5. Heat an *appam* wok or a deep non-stick griddle and grease lightly with oil. Pour one big spoonful of the batter into it.

6. Using a wooden spoon, slowly rotate the batter on the griddle so that a thin layer forms on the sides while the middle remains thick. Cover and cook for 1 minute. The middle part should become fluffy.

7. Repeat for the remaining batter. Serve hot with vegetable stew.

AVIAL

(Mixed vegetables in curry)

INGREDIENTS

Raw banana, peeled and cut into pieces	1
Drumsticks, cut into 2" pieces	2
White pumpkin, peeled and chopped	1 cup
Carrot, peeled and cut into pieces	2
Beans, cut into pieces	a few
Curd	1 cup
Salt	to taste
Turmeric powder	½ tsp
Grated coconut	2 cups
Green chillies	4-5
Curry leaves	few
Coconut oil	2 tbsp
Oil	2 tbsp
Cumin seeds	¼ tsp
Whole red chilli	1

METHOD

1. Cook the vegetables with salt and turmeric powder, in a little oil.

2. Grind the coconut and green chillies with a little water. Mix this paste with the cooked vegetables.

3. Add 1 cup of water and curry leaves to the above mixture, boil and simmer for 5 minutes.

4. Serve hot garnished with heated coconut oil, along with cumin seeds and whole red chilli.

ALLEPPY POTATO CURRY

INGREDIENTS

Potatoes	3, medium
Coconut	1
Raw mangoes, boiled and pureed	2
Green chillies	4
Red chilli powder	1 tbsp
Curry leaves	few
Salt	to taste
Oil	for deep-frying/2-3 cups

METHOD

1. Peel the potatoes, cut into cubes and deep-fry. Keep aside.
2. Grind grated coconut and red chilli powder in a grinder to form a smooth thick paste.
3. Dilute with a little water and cook well with salt.
4. Add raw mangoes, curry leaves and green chillies. Add two cups of water. Cook and bring to a boil.
5. Cook the potatoes in the above gravy well until soft or for 10-15 minutes.
6. Serve hot with plain rice.

PAAL PAYASAM

(Rice pudding)

INGREDIENTS

Rice	½ cup
Milk	5 cups
Cardamom powder	1 tsp
Clarified butter/*Ghee*	1 tbsp
Cashewnuts	7-8
Raisins	few

METHOD

1. Wash the rice and soak in water for 30 minutes.
2. Drain and cook rice in milk until soft. Keep stirring till the milk thickens. Add cardamom powder and sugar, and stir until sugar is dissolved. Keep aside.
3. In a pan, heat *ghee* and fry cashewnuts till they are golden brown. Add the raisins and sauté for 1 minute.
4. Pour on the rice mixture and serve warm.

TAMIL MENU

Toor Dal Rasam
Vendaikai Avial
Mooru Kolambu with Vadai
Katrikai Ennai Kai
Curd Rice
Idiappam
Cashewnut Halwa

TOOR DAL RASAM
(Tangy red gram soup)

INGREDIENTS

Split red gram (*toor dal*)	½ cup
Water	3-4 cups
Turmeric powder	¼ tsp
Black pepper	½ tsp
Cumin seeds	1 tsp
Tamarind	1 small ball
Garlic (optional)	4 cloves
Salt	to taste

FOR SEASONING:

Ghee/Refined oil	1 tbsp
Mustard seeds	¼ tsp
Curry leaves	few
Coriander leaves, finely chopped	few

METHOD

1. Cook the *dal* in 3 cups of water with turmeric powder and salt. Churn into a paste and keep aside.
2. Add ¼ cup of water to the tamarind and squeeze out the pulpy liquid.
3. Coarsely grind black pepper, cumin seeds and garlic.
4. Heat oil in a pan and add mustard seeds. When they start to crackle, add the coarsely ground spices and fry.
5. Add tamarind juice and curry leaves. Boil and cook for 5 minutes. Add *dal*.
6. Garnish with finely chopped coriander leaves and serve hot.

VENDAIKAI AVIAL

(Lady's fingers in coconut curry)

INGREDIENTS

Lady's fingers	12
Baby Onions	½ cup
Green chillies, chopped	3
Dry red chillies	4
Garlic, chopped (optional)	2 tbsp
Cumin seeds	1½ tsp
Grated coconut	½ a coconut
Turmeric powder	¼ tsp
Salt	to taste
Curry leaves	few
Sesame oil	¼ cup
Mustard seed	¼ tsp
Black gram (*urad dal*), soaked in water	¼ tsp
Oil	for cooking and deep-frying

METHOD

1. Wash, dry and cut the lady's fingers in 1" pieces. Deep-fry and keep aside.
2. Grind chilli, cumin seeds, and coconut separately and keep aside.
3. Heat oil in pan, add mustard seeds, black gram and curry leaves. Fry until brown and add onions, red chillies, garlic, turmeric powder, and green chillies. Fry again for 5 minutes.

4. Add lady's fingers, ground spices, coconut, salt and a little water.

5. Keep stirring till the mixture boils. Cover and cook till the vegetables are soft.

6. Serve hot.

Mooru Kolambu with Vadai

(Curd curry with vada)

INGREDIENTS FOR VADA:

Oil	2 cups
Black gram (*urad dal*), washed	1 cup
Salt	to taste
Green chillies, chopped	2
Coriander leaves, chopped	few
Ginger, chopped	1 tbsp
Asafoetida (*hing*)	a pinch

FOR CURRY:

Sour curd	2 cups
Refined oil/vegetable oil	1 tbsp
Grated coconut	1 cup
Mustard seeds	¼ tsp
Fenugreek seeds	¼ tsp
Curry leaves	few
Dry red chillies	2
Salt	to taste
Turmeric powder	¼ tsp
Green chillies, slit into half	2-3

METHOD

1. Soak *urad dal* overnight. Drain the water completely and grind *dal* with salt and asafoetida.

2. Add chopped green chillies, coriander leaves and ginger to the *dal* and mix well.

3. Make small walnut-sized balls out of the mixture, deep-fry on medium flame till golden brown. Put them in cold water for 3 minutes, squeeze excess water and keep ready to immerse in curry.

METHOD

1. For curry, heat oil and add mustard and fenugreek seeds, curry leaves and green chillies. After 2 minutes add beaten curd, along with two cups of water, stirring constantly.

2. Add salt, turmeric powder and keep on the slow fire for 5 minutes. Add grated coconut, vadas and bring to a boil.

3. Separately, heat oil and dry red chillies and curry leaves. Sprinkle on the curry and serve hot.

Katrikai Ennai Kai

(Brinjal in oil)

INGREDIENTS

Brinjals (green or purple)	12 (small with stalk)
Onions, sliced	2
Garlic, chopped	10 cloves
Oil	¾ cup
Ginger	1" piece
Chilli powder	1 tsp
Coriander powder	2 tbsp
Tamarind pulp	¼ cup
Sambhar powder	1 tbsp
Cloves	2
Cinnamon, broken into pieces	1 long stick
Coconut, ground into paste	¼ cup
Cashewnuts, ground into paste	10
Curry leaves	few
Whole red chillies	2

METHOD

1. Slit the brinjals into 4 with the stalks intact and immerse in cold water.

2. Heat oil in a vessel, add cloves, cinnamon, sliced onions, garlic and fry for sometime. Add brinjals, salt, chilli powder, sambhar powder, and coriander powder. Sprinkle some water and cover and cook.

3. When brinjals are half done, add coconut paste, tamarind pulp, cashewnut paste and cook till tender.

4. Separately, heat 1 tbsp of oil and fry curry leaves and whole red chillies. Garnish on the brinjal and serve hot.

Curd Rice

INGREDIENTS

Rice, boiled	2 cups
Beaten curd	1 cup
Salt	to taste
Green chillies, chopped	2
Coriander leaves, chopped	a few
Mustard seeds	1 tsp
Whole red chillies	2
Oil	1 tbsp
Black gram (*urad dal*), washed	½ tsp
Curry leaves	few

METHOD

1. Mix curd with cooled boiled rice and add salt. Keep aside.

2. Heat oil in a pan and add mustard seeds. As it starts crackling, add *urad dal*. When *dal* turns brown, add green chillies, whole red chillies and curry leaves. After 1 minute, pour this on the curd rice.

3. Garnish with coriander leaves and serve cold.

IDIAPPAM

(Fluffy rice bread)

INGREDIENTS

Rice	½ cup
Salt	to taste
Coconut slivers	a few
Soda powder	a pinch

METHOD

1. Soak rice in water for 6 hours. Drain and dry the rice. Pound the rice and sift the flour. (It is better if you use the dry blade of the grinder for pounding).

2. In 1 cup of boiling water, add soda powder, salt and riceflour and make a thick dough. Make dough-balls and press them through an idiappam press and steam in a pressure cooker.

3. Add coconut slivers on top and serve. This tastes better when eaten with curries.

Note: Idiappam press is available in all kitchenware stores.

CASHEWNUT HALWA

(Cashewnut dessert)

INGREDIENTS

Cashewnut paste	2 cups
Semolina (*suji*)	2 tbsp
Sugar	½ cup
Ghee	½ cup
Raisins	2 tbsp
Water	½ cup

METHOD

1. Grind the cashewnuts into a paste. Fry the semolina in 2 tsp of *ghee* till it becomes brown.

2. Mix the fried semolina with cashewnut paste.

3. Add ½ cup of hot water to the sugar and make it into a thin sticky syrup.

4. Add the cashewnut and semolina paste to the syrup and stir constantly on slow fire.

5. Gradually add *ghee* in little amounts. Add raisins and keep stirring till the mixture thickens.

6. Serve hot.

Soorana Chi Koshimbir
Panch-dali Chi Amti
Bhendi Chi Khatta Meetha
Masale Bhat
Thali Peeth
Puranchi Poli

SOORANA CHI KOSHIMBIR

(Spiced yam salad)

INGREDIENTS

Yam, chopped into pieces	1 ½ cups
Juice	of 2 lemons
Fresh coconut, grated	¾ cup
Onions, chopped	2
Coriander leaves, chopped	2 tbsp
Salt	to taste
Sugar	½ tsp
Green chillies, chopped	4
Oil	2 cups
Tomatoes, cut into squares	2
Capsicum, cut into squares	1
Asafoetida (*hing*)	a pinch
Mustard Seeds	½ tsp

METHOD

1. Clean wash and peel the skin of the yam and dice it into ¼" cubes. Marinate for ten to fifteen minutes with a little salt and 2 tsp of lime juice.

2. Deep-fry the cubes till they are well done and turn golden brown. Drain excess oil, remove from heat and set aside.

3. In a bowl, mix grated coconut, chopped coriander leaves, lime juice, chopped onions, green chillies, salt, sugar, tomatoes and capsicum.

4. Heat 2 tsp of oil in a wok, fry mustard seeds and a pinch of asafoetida in it. As the mustard seeds begin to crackle, pour this seasoning over the coconut-spice mixture and set aside.

5. Mix the fried yam with the above mixture. Garnish with more coriander leaves, grated coconut. Serve when cool.

PANCH-DALI CHI AMTI

(Five-lentil gravy)

INGREDIENTS

Lentil (*masoor dal*)	¼ cup
Bengal gram (*chana dal*)	4 tbsp
Washed black gram (*urad dal*)	2 tbsp
Dry cocum flowers, soaked	2-3 (optional)
Mustard seeds	1 tsp
Turmeric powder	½ tsp
Asafoetida (*hing*)	a pinch
Salt	to taste
Jaggery	1 tsp
Onions, chopped	2
Oil	3 tbsp
Curry leaves	few
Green chillies, chopped	6-8
Lime juice	4 tbsp
Coriander leaves, chopped	few

METHOD

1. Clean and wash the *dals* and soak them together for about 15 minutes.
2. Pressure-cook the *dals* with salt and turmeric powder till the cooker gives out 2-3 whistles.
3. Add jaggery and cocum to the cooked *dal* and keep aside.
4. Heat oil in a pan and add asafoetida, mustard seeds and curry leaves. Wait till the mustard seeds start to crackle.
5. Add chopped green chillies and onions. Fry till onions become golden brown.
6. Mix *dal* in the onion masala and add some water if required. Garnish with coriander leaves and serve hot.

BHENDI CHI KHATTA MEETHA

(Sweet and sour lady's finger)

INGREDIENTS

Lady's finger	½ kg/ 2½ cups chopped
Oil	4 tbsp
Tamarind pulp	2 tbsp
Asafoetida (*hing*)	a pinch
Jaggery	1 tbsp
Salt	to taste
Mustard seeds	½ tsp
Turmeric powder	½ tsp
Green chillies, cut lengthwise	5-6
Coriander leaves, chopped	few
Curry leaves	few

METHOD

1. Wash and dry the lady's fingers. Chop them into ¾" pieces.
2. Heat oil in a wok and add asafoetida, mustard seeds, curry leaves, green chillies and turmeric powder.
3. Add the lady's finger and fry till it is done. This should take at least 10-15 minutes on high flame.
4. Add tamarind pulp and jaggery and mix well.
5. Garnish with chopped coriander leaves and serve hot.

MASALE BHAT

(Spicy rice with vegetables)

INGREDIENTS

Basmati Rice	1 cup
Coriander seeds	1 tsp
Cumin seeds	1 tsp
Mustard seeds	½ tsp
Cashewnuts	10-12
Red chilli powder	1 tsp
Cloves	4-5
Turmeric powder	½ tsp
Cinnamon	2-3 pieces
Asafoetida	a pinch
Green chillies	2-3
Salt	to taste
Yogurt	1 tbsp
Oil	2 tbsp
Fresh coconut, grated	2-3 tbsp
Fresh coriander leaves, chopped	¼ cup
Mixed vegetables chopped	1 cup
(cauliflower, beans, carrot, peas and eggplant)	
Lime juice	2 tbsp
Clarified butter/ghee	1 tsp

METHOD

1. Grind coriander seeds, cumin seeds, cloves and cinnamon into powder.
2. Clean and wash the rice and soak in water for 20 minutes.
3. Heat oil in a deep-bottomed pan and add the mustard seeds, asafoetida and turmeric powder.
4. Sauté the vegetables in this seasoning for about 5 minutes.
5. Add cashewnuts, green chillies, salt, red chilli powder, ground spices, yogurt and the rice and mix well.
6. Add boiling water to the above mixture and cover and cook till the rice is done.

(Water should be double the rice quantity i.e. 2 cups).

7. Add lime juice to the rice. Garnish the rice with coriander leaves and grated coconut. Serve with a spoonful of ghee.

THALI PEETH

(Mixed flour bread)

INGREDIENTS

Jowar flour	½ cup
Wheatflour (atta)	½ cup
Riceflour	½ cup
Salt	to taste
Coriander seeds	2 tbsp
Bengal gram (chana dal)	4 tbsp
Fenugreek seeds	½ tsp
Black gram (urad dal)	4 tbsp
Water	for kneading

METHOD

1. Dry roast coriander seeds, Bengal gram, fenugreek seeds, and urad dal on a griddle.
2. Set aside to cool. When cooled, grind together to make a flour.
3. Mix all the flours and the above mixture. Add salt and make a dough using enough water. Knead well.
4. Divide the dough into 7-8 balls. On a non-stick surface, flatten the balls into circular discs, using a rolling pin gently.
5. Heat another griddle and spread a thin layer of oil over it. When the oil becomes hot, cook a thalipeeth (the flat circle you have just made) on it till it browns from both sides. Repeat for all the discs.
6. Serve hot with pickle.

PURANCHI POLI

(Bread stuffed with Bengal gram and jaggery)

INGREDIENTS

FOR THE DOUGH:

Cakeflour (self-raising)	2 cups
Oil	¼ cup

FOR THE FILLING:

Bengal gram (*chana dal*)	1 cup
Cardamoms, powdered	2-3
Sugar	1 cup
Salt	a pinch
Saffron, soaked	a few strands
Jaggery	½ cup
Nutmeg, powdered	a pinch

METHOD

FOR THE DOUGH:

1. Cook the Bengal gram in a pressure cooker with water 2½ times the volume of the gram, till soft.
2. When cool, blend in a blender or grind to a thick paste.
3. Add sugar and/or jaggery.
4. Add salt, saffron and nutmeg. Mix well. Cook in a heavy-bottomed pan on medium heat till the mixture becomes thick and firm but remains moist.
5. Remove from flame and cool.
6. Make about 15-20 balls with this filling.

FOR THE POLIS:

1. Divide the dough set aside earlier into 15-20 portions and make dough balls. Stretch out or flatten a ball of dough on your palm, stuff with a ball of filling and gently seal the dough-ball, taking enough care not to leave any gaps for the filling to seep out.
2. Repeat for the rest of the dough and the filling. Keep the balls covered with a thin muslin cloth so that they do not dry.
3. Lightly flour a rolling board. Gently and uniformly roll the stuffed dough-balls into a thin, small pancake-type *poli*.
4. Ensure that the stuffing doesn't leak out of the cover as you roll. Meanwhile heat a griddle.
5. When it is hot, place a *poli* on it and dry roast till it is soft and golden on both sides. The *poli* should be soft and flaky. Serve hot, smeared with *ghee*.
6. If you want to store them, cool them first. Then cover with a clean, soft muslin cloth and store in a flat, round airtight box.

KASHMIRI MENU

Nadur Roganjosh
Barith Marchavangun
Chaman Olu
Steamed Rice with Dry Fruits
Naan
Doon Chetin
Phirni

NADUR ROGANJOSH

(Lotus root curry in Kashmiri masala)

INGREDIENTS

Lotus root	500 gm/2 cups (sliced & parboiled)
Oil	5 tbsp
Cumin seeds	½ tsp
Cloves	3-4
Bay leaves	2
Black cardamoms, crushed	2
Salt	to taste
Asafoetida	a pinch
Red chilli powder	1 tsp
Yogurt	2 tbsp
Ginger powder (*saunth*)	1 tsp
Aniseed powder (*saunf*)	½ tsp
Garam masala powder	½ tsp

METHOD

1. Cut the lotus root into 2" long pieces and further cut those into halves. Wash well.

2. Heat oil in a heavy-bottomed pan, add cumin seeds, cloves, bay leaves and black cardamoms; stir till they crackle.

3. Add the lotus root pieces, salt and asafoetida. Sauté over low heat for about 7-10 minutes. Stir constantly to make sure that the mixture does not stick to the bottom.

4. Mix red chilli powder with the yogurt and add to the mixture. Stir vigorously for 30 seconds over high flame. Add ½ cup of water.

5. Bring to a boil, add ginger, aniseed and *garam masala* powders. Cook for 10-15 minutes or till the water dries. Serve hot.

BARITH MARCHAVANGUN

(Stuffed green chillies)

INGREDIENTS

Large size green chillies	10-15
Vinegar	½ cup
Walnuts, shelled	¾ cup
Ginger, grated	2 tbsp
Pomegranate seeds	3½ tsp
Cumin seeds	1 tsp
Asafoetida (*hing*)	a pinch
Salt	to taste
Water	a few tbsp
Oil for frying	½ cup

METHOD

1. Wash the chillies and make a small slit in each. Deseed and soak them in vinegar for at least 1 hour.

2. Grind the walnuts, ginger, pomegranate seeds, cumin seeds, asafoetida and salt to a smooth paste with a little water.

3. Remove the chillies from vinegar and spread out on a plate. Fill the slits with a little of the ground paste. Do not overstuff,

1. Anardana
2. Cinnamons sticks
3. White til
4. Cumin seeds
5. Fennel seeds
6. Black pepper
7. Black cardamoms
8. Bay leaves
9. Fenugreek seed
10. Whole red chilli
11. Whole coriander
12. Star aniseed
13. Carom seeds
14. Cloves
15. Cardamom
16. Mustard seeds
17. Cocum flower
18. Khus Khus
19. Nigella seed (Kalonji)
20. Tamarind

1. Channa dal
2. Whole urad dal
3. Rajmah
4. Washed moong dal
5. Washed urad dal
6. Split moong dal
7. Washed masoor dal
8. Black channa
9. Whole moong dal
10. Whole masoor dal
11. Split urad dal
12. Brown whole dal (Moth)
13. Toor dal
14. Kabuli channa
15. Red rice
16. Corn

Rajasthani Menu
Rajasthani dal, Chokha, Baingan Bhurta, Churma, Gatte Ki Sabji, Rabri, Batti

Karnataka Menu
Raagi Roti, Chitraana, Sevian, Payasam, Kosumbari, Sambhar

Punjabi Menu
Pindi Chhole, Punjabi Kadhi, Bhatoora along with white butter

Kerala Menu
Vegetable Stew, Alleppy Potato Curry, Avial, Paal Payasam and Appam

put only enough so as to allow the slits to remain closed. Keep aside.

4. Heat oil in a pan. Shallow-fry the chillies (about a minute) over low flame till they change colour. Serve as a side dish.

Chaman Olu

(Cottage cheese and potatoes)

INGREDIENTS

Cottage cheese (*paneer*)	8 pieces cut into 2"-sized pieces
Potatoes, peeled	2-3
Oil	1 cup (for frying)
Water	1½ cup
Turmeric powder	1 tsp
Ginger powder	1 tsp
Aniseed powder	2 tsp
Asafoetida (*hing*)	a pinch
Salt	to taste
Black cardamoms, crushed	2
Yogurt	3 tbsp
Milk	3 tbsp
Clarified butter (*ghee*)	2 tbsp
Cloves	3-4
Green cardamoms, crushed	3
Green chillies, sliced	2

METHOD

1. Heat oil and fry the cottage cheese pieces until they become golden brown. Transfer pieces to a pot of water.

2. Cut the potatoes into ½" thick rounds. Fry and keep aside.

3. Place the pot with the cottage cheese and water over a high flame. Add turmeric, ginger, aniseed powder, asafoetida, salt,

black cardamoms and potatoes. Cook until the gravy is reduced to half.

4. Mix yogurt and milk together and add to the above mixture. Bring to a boil, stirring continuously for 5 minutes and then remove from the flame.

5. In a pan, heat the clarified butter and sauté the cloves and green cardamoms. Add this to the preparation. Garnish with green chillies and serve.

Steamed Rice with Dry Fruits

INGREDIENTS

Rice, cooked	2 cups
Clarified butter/*Ghee*	2 tbsp
Mixed dry fruit (cashewnuts, almond, raisins, pistachios)	½ cup

METHOD

1. Heat *ghee* in a pan and add all the dry fruits.

2. Mix in rice and stir well.

3. Serve hot.

Naan

(Roasted fluffy flour bread)

INGREDIENTS

Refined flour	4 cups
Milk	1 cup
Baking powder	1 tsp
Water	as required
Baking soda (soda bi-carbonate)	½ tsp
Oil	2 tbsp

Salt	1 tsp
Onion seeds	2 tsp
Egg	1
Sugar	2 tsp
Butter	2 tsp
Yogurt	2 tbsp

METHOD

1. Sieve flour with baking powder, baking soda and salt. Add sugar, egg, milk, yogurt and water. Knead well into a medium-soft dough.
2. Apply a little oil and keep the dough under a wet cloth for one hour.
3. Make eight equal portions of the dough. Apply a little oil and roll each part into a flat circle. Stretch from one side to give a triangular shape. Sprinkle onion seeds on one side.
4. Roast them in a pre-heated oven or a pre-heated *tandoor* (barbecue grill) till they become golden brown on both sides.
5. Serve hot, topped with butter.

DOON CHETIN

(Walnut chutney)

INGREDIENTS

Walnuts shelled	½ cup
Onions, chopped	½ cup
Green chillies, chopped	2
Yogurt	½ cup
Red chilli powder	¼ tsp
Salt	to taste

METHOD

Grind all the ingredients together to a paste and serve chilled.

PHIRNI

(Kashmiri rice pudding)

INGREDIENTS

Rice	¾ cup
Milk	5 cups
Green cardamoms, crushed	4
Almonds, blanched and shredded	3½ tbsp
Pistachios, chopped	few
Saffron	a few strands
Sugar	1 cup
Edible silver paper (*varak*)	6 pieces
Clay bowls (soaked in water)	6

METHOD

1. Pick, clean and wash the rice. Soak in water for 1 hour. Drain and let the rice dry. When dry, either crumble rice or grind coarsely for 10 seconds.
2. Heat milk in a heavy-bottomed pot. Bring to a boil and add the rice, green cardamoms and almonds. Stir frequently with a ladle.
3. Lower the flame and cook till the rice gets soft and the milk thickens. Stir frequently to ensure that it doesn't stick to the bottom.
4. Crush the saffron and soak in a few spoons of hot milk. Add saffron and sugar to the rice and stir. Remove from flame.
5. Remove the clay bowls from the water, and allow them to dry. When the *phirun* is ready, pour into the separate bowls. Decorate with silver leaves and chopped pistachios and serve chilled.

Narkel Chhola Dal
Begun Bhaja
Kathal Alu Tarkari
Bori Diya Palan Saag
Ghee Bhat
Luchi
Rasamalai
Tomato Khajoor Chutney

NARKEL CHHOLA DAL

(Bengal gram with coconut)

INGREDIENTS

Bengal gram (*chana dal*)	200 gm/1 cup
Turmeric powder	1 tsp
Oil	2 tbsp
Aniseed	2 tsp
Cinnamon stick	1-2
Fresh coconut, thin small pieces	4 tsp
Salt	1 tsp
Sugar	1 tsp
Bay leaves	2-3
Ginger paste	2 tbsp
Red whole chillies	4-5

METHOD

1. Boil the Bengal gram with turmeric powder, salt, bay leaves, and water till done.
2. Heat oil separately in a pan and sauté aniseed, cinnamon, ginger paste and coconut pieces. Fry for 5 minutes.
3. Add the boiled gram and cook for 10 minutes.
4. Mix in the sugar.

5. Heat 1 tbsp oil separately, add red chillies and sauté. Pour this seasoning on the *dal*, and serve hot.

BEGUN BHAJA

(Fried eggplant pieces)

INGREDIENTS

Large eggplant/brinjal, cut into quarters	250 gm/2½ cups
Salt	2 tsp
Turmeric powder	2 tsp
Mustard oil	4 tbsp
Red chilli powder	1 tsp
Lime juice	½ tsp
Coriander leaves, chopped	a few

METHOD

1. Rub the eggplant pieces with salt, turmeric and red chilli powder. Keep aside for 15 minutes.
2. Heat mustard oil in a shallow pan and fry the egglplant pieces till golden brown in colour.
3. Drain excess oil and keep aside.
4. Serve hot with rice and *Narkel Chhola Dal*.

Kathal Alu Tarkari

(Jackfruit and potato curry)

INGREDIENTS

Jackfruit (*kathal*), diced	2 cups
Potatoes, peeled and cut into cubes	2
Mustard oil	3 tbsp
Onions, chopped	1
Ginger paste	1 tsp
Garlic paste	1 tsp
Turmeric powder	½ tsp
Coriander powder	2 tsp
Red chilli powder	1 tsp
Cumin seed powder	1½ tsp
Tomatoes, chopped	3-4
Salt	to taste
Water	4 cups
Oil	for deep-frying
Coriander leaves, chopped	2 tbsp
Garam masala powder	½ tsp
Sugar	½ tsp

METHOD

1. Heat oil in a wok and add the jackfruit and potatoes. Sauté for 10-12 minutes and keep aside.

2. Heat mustard oil, add cumin seeds, onions, ginger-garlic paste and sauté for 5 minutes.

3. Now add the tomatoes and cook till the oil separates from the sides of the wok. Add all the spices and sugar and fry for 5 minutes.

4. Add jackfruit, potatoes, salt and water. Cook till the vegetables are tender.

5. Garnish with *garam masala* powder and coriander leaves and serve hot.

Bori Diya Palan Saag

(Vadi with spinach)

INGREDIENTS

Spinach, chopped	2½ cups
Vadi	1 cup
Oil	2 tbsp
Bay leaves	2
Turmeric powder	1 tsp
Water	¼ cup
Salt	to taste
Sugar	2 tsp
Red chilli powder	1 tsp

METHOD

1. Heat oil in a pan; fry the *vadis* and keep aside.

2. In the same oil, add bay leaves, turmeric powder and spinach. Fry for 2 minutes.

3. Add water and *vadi* along with salt, red chilli powder and sugar. Cook till the water dries up and the spinach is done.

4. Serve hot.

Note: Vadis *are available in the market.*

Ghee Bhat

(Rice with clarified butter)

INGREDIENTS

Basmati rice, cooked	2 cups
Clarified butter/*Ghee*	3 tbsp
Cloves	4
Cinnamon	2
Bay leaves	2
Black peppercorns	3-4
Salt	1 tsp

METHOD

1. Heat the clarified butter, sauté the cloves, cinnamon, bay leaves and peppercorns for a few seconds.
2. Add the rice and sauté for 1 minute.
3. Add salt and serve hot.

Luchi

(Deep-fried flour bread)

INGREDIENTS

Refined flour	5 cups
Clarified butter/*Ghee*	¼ cup
Oil	for deep-frying
Salt	½ tsp
Water	½ cup

METHOD

1. Make a stiff dough with flour, salt, *ghee* and water. Keep aside for 15-20 minutes.
2. Separate the dough into small round lemon-sized balls.
3. Roll out the balls into flat discs, about 4" in diameter.
4. Heat oil for frying, deep-fry the discs till golden brown in colour.
5. Serve hot with *Narkel Chhola Dal*.

Rasamalai

(Cottage cheese dumplings in thick creamy milk)

INGREDIENTS

Cottage cheese (*chhena*)	250 gm / 2½ cups grated
Semolina	1 tsp
Sugar	3 cups
Water	2½ cups
Milk	7 cups
Cardamom powder	2 tsp
Pistachios, ground	4 tsp
Saffron	a few strands

METHOD

1. Knead the cottage cheese well with the semolina till the dough is light and fluffy. Divide and shape into small round lemon-sized balls.
2. Make a thick sugar syrup with water. Keep aside.
3. Flatten the balls to make patties and then poach them in the thick syrup for 15 minutes.
4. Bring the milk to a boil and cook until it is reduced to three-quarters of the original quantity. Add the remaining sugar, saffron and cardamom powder. Stir till the sugar dissolves completely.
5. Add the poached patties to the hot milk. Remove from the flame and cool.
6. Serve chilled, garnished with chopped pistachios.

Note: Poach: Cooking gently in water or flavoured liquid at a temperature just below boiling point.

TOMATO KHAJOOR CHUTNEY

(Tomato and date chutney)

INGREDIENTS

Tomatoes, chopped	5 cups
Dates, chopped	¼ cup
Oil	2 tsp
Mustard seeds	1 tsp
Dry red chillies	2-3
Red chilli powder	½ tsp
Sugar	2 tbsp
Salt	to taste

METHOD

1. Heat oil and add the mustard seeds and dry red chillies. Sauté for a few seconds, till the mustard seeds crackle.

2. Add the tomatoes and cook for 15 minutes. Add sugar and salt; stir till the sugar dissolves completely.

3. Cook till the mixture obtains a thick consistency. Mix in the dates at the end.

4. Serve after it cools. When refrigerated, this chutney can last up to 2-3 days.

Dal Masoor
Masala Potatoes
Mushroom Balchao
Sanas
Vegetable Curry
Special Goan Cakes

DAL MASOOR

(Goan lentil)

INGREDIENTS

Whole lentil (*masoor dal*)	1 cup
Tomatoes	3
Red chillies	4
Cumin seeds	1 tbsp
Coriander seeds	1 tsp
Turmeric powder	½ tsp
Garlic, chopped	4 flakes
Onions, sliced	2
Salt	to taste
Tomato puree	1 cup
Lime juice	1 tbsp
Cocum flowers	4-5

METHOD

1. Grind red chillies, cumin and coriander seeds to a fine paste.
2. Wash the *dal* and soak in 3 cups of water for 15-20 minutes. Heat 3 tbsp oil and fry onions, tomatoes and garlic till soft. Mix in the ground paste and fry for 5 more minutes.
3. And salt, turmeric powder and *dal* along with the water in which it was soaked. Bring to a boil, reduce heat to simmer and add cleaned and washed cocums.
4. Cook till done. Add lime juice and serve hot with plain boiled rice.

MASALA POTATOES

(Spicy potatoes)

INGREDIENTS

Potatoes, peeled and cubed	2½ cups
Onion	1 large
Tomatoes, peeled and chopped	2
Salt	to taste
Sugar	a pinch
Whole red chillies	4
Cumin seeds	½ tsp
Garlic flakes	4
Ginger	½" piece
Coriander leaves	a few
Oil	3 tbsp

FOR GARNISH:

Onion slices, crisply fried	1 onion
Cashewnuts and raisins, fried	1 tbsp

METHOD

1. Grind garlic, ginger, red chillies, coriander leaves and onion to a paste.
2. Heat oil in a pan and add cumin seeds. When they turn brown, add the above paste and fry for 5-6 minutes.
3. Add tomatoes and fry till they are soft.
4. Add potatoes and mix well. Add sugar and salt. Add 1 cup of water. Cover and cook till mixture dries and potatoes become tender.
5. Serve garnished with fried onions, cashewnuts and raisins.

MUSHROOM BALCHAO

(Tangy mushroom flavoured with chillies)

INGREDIENTS

Mushrooms	500 gm (1 packet)
Vinegar	¼ cup
Red chillies	6
Onions	4 (medium)
Garlic	8-10 flakes
Ginger	1" piece
Cumin seeds	2 tsp
Peppercorns	½ tbsp
Green chillies, slit	1 tbsp
Curry leaves	a few sprigs
Turmeric powder	½ tsp
Salt	to taste
Oil	6 tbsp

METHOD

1. Grind all the whole spices, red chillies and garlic.

2. Marinate the mushrooms in salt, vinegar, and turmeric powder for half an hour. Heat 3 tbsp oil and fry the ginger and onions to a light golden colour.

3. Add the mushrooms and the rest of the ingredients. Cook till tender and dry. Serve hot with rice.

SANAS

(Fluffy Goan rice bread)

INGREDIENTS

Riceflour	250 gm/1½ cups
Coconut milk	1 cup
Yeast	2 tbsp
Salt	to taste
Sugar	½ tsp
Baking soda powder	a pinch

METHOD

1. Mix all the above ingredients in a batter and keep aside for ½ an hour. Grease cups of an *idli* stand. Place one large cup of water in a pressure cooker.

2. Fill the *idli* stand cups with the batter and place the stand in the cup of water in the cooker. Close the lid but do not use the pressure regulator for making *sanas*. They will be ready within 15 minutes.

3. Serve hot with curry.

VEGETABLE CURRY

INGREDIENTS

Mixed vegetables, sliced (carrots, French beans etc.)	2 cups
Coconut, grated	½
Mint leaves	1 cup
Coriander leaves, chopped	1 cup
Green chillies, chopped	3
Ginger	½ inch piece
Garlics flake	4
Cumin seeds, ground	1 tsp
Coriander powder	1 tbsp
Turmeric powder	½ tsp
Tamarind juice	20 tsp
Onion, minced	1, large
Tomatoes, sliced	2
Salt	to taste
Chilli powder	to taste
Oil	4 tbsp

METHOD

1. Grind coconut, ginger, garlic, green chillies, mint and coriander leaves to a paste.
2. Heat 4 tbsp of oil and fry the onions till soft. Add the vegetables and fry for 2 minutes. Put in tomatoes and coconut paste. Add all spices. Cook till tomatoes and vegetables are almost done.
3. Add tamarind juice and 2 cups of water. When the vegetables are tender, remove from fire and serve with boiled rice.

SPECIAL GOAN CAKES

INGREDIENTS

Semolina	2 cups
Eggs	3
Sugar	1½ cups
Caraway seeds	1 tbsp
Salt	to taste
Butter	2 tbsp

METHOD

1. Roast the semolina on a griddle without butter to a golden colour.
2. With 1 cup of water and sugar, prepare a thick syrup. Cool the syrup.
3. Grind the coconut to a paste.
4. Separate the eggs. Keep the yolks aside.
5. Beat the yolks and mix with the cooled sugar syrup. Mix in the remaining ingredients including semolina. Beat the mixture into a dough.
6. Divide the dough into small, round and flat cakes. Arrange on greased tray and bake in a moderate oven till done.
7. Cut into small pieces and serve.

MUGHLAI MENU

Malai Matar Shorba
Potato Salad
Dal Makhani
Shahi Paneer
Gobi Mussallam
Kandahari Naan
Handi Biryani
Bhurani
Bundi Ladoo

MALAI MATAR SHORBA

(Cream of green peas soup)

INGREDIENTS

Peas, shelled	1½ cups
Carrot, chopped	1 small
Onion, sliced	¼
Salt, pepper, cinnamon, cloves	to taste
Bay leaves	2
Butter	½ tsp
Cornflour	½ tsp
Milk	6 tbsp
Bread	½ slice
Cream	1tbsp
Oil	for frying croutons

METHOD

1. Boil the peas, carrot and onion with the whole spices and the bay leaves in four cups of water.
2. When tender, mash and strain.
3. Prepare white sauce with butter, cornflour and milk as shown in the Basic Recipes section.
4. Add the vegetable puree to the white sauce. Add salt and pepper.
5. Serve hot with bread croutons and garnished with cream.

POTATO SALAD

INGREDIENTS

Potatoes, boiled peeled and cut into cubes	4
Dill leaves, chopped	1 tbsp
Hung curd	½ cup
Salt	to taste
Black pepper	1 tsp
Tabasco sauce	1 tsp
Castor sugar	1 tsp

METHOD

1. Chill the potatoes in the refrigerator for 15 minutes.
2. Mix all the ingredients and serve cold.

DAL MAKHANI

(Thick creamy black gram in curry)

INGREDIENTS

Whole black gram (*urad dal*)	¾ cup
Red kidney beans (*rajmah*)	1 tbsp
Ginger paste	2 tbsp
Garlic paste	2 tbsp
Onion paste	2 tbsp
Tomatoes, boiled, peeled, pureed	2
Salt	to taste
Red chilli powder	1 tsp
Coriander powder	2 tsp
Dry mango powder (*amchur*)	1 tsp
Oil	2 tbsp
Cream	½ cup
Butter	1 tbsp
Sugar	½ tsp

METHOD

1. Wash the *dal* and *rajmah*. Soak together for 4-5 hours or overnight. Put soaked *dal*, ½ tsp of ginger, garlic and salt in a pressure cooker. Add sufficient quantity of water and pressure-cook for 15 minutes.

2. Heat oil and fry onion paste till brown, add ginger and garlic pastes and then tomato puree. Fry till the oil separates.

3. Add all the spices and fry for 5 minutes. Add *dal* to this mixture, bring to a boil, and cook for 10 minutes. Add water if required.

4. Add cream to the *dal*. Garnish with butter and serve hot.

SHAHI PANEER

(Cottage cheese in rich gravy)

INGREDIENTS

Cottage cheese/*paneer*, cubed	1½ cups
Onions, chopped	2 cups
Tomatoes, chopped	2 cups
Garlic, chopped	2 tbsp
Ginger, chopped	2 tbsp
Clarified butter/*ghee*	for frying paneer
Salt, red chilli, turmeric and garam masala powders	to taste
Coriander leaves	a few
Fresh cream	4-5 tbsp

METHOD

1. Heat *ghee* in a wok and fry the *paneer* cubes till they turn light brown. Keep aside.

2. Grind onion, ginger and garlic to a paste.

3. Cut the tomato into small pieces and blend to a puree.

4. Heat *ghee* in a heavy-bottomed pan and fry the onion, garlic and ginger pastes to golden brown till the oil separates.

5. Add salt, red chilli and turmeric powders, and tomato puree. Fry with the help of a little water till the spices look done and the oil separates.

6. Add fried *paneer* cubes and fry a little more. Add cream.

7. Add sufficient water and cook covered till curry is done.

8. Serve hot, sprinkled with *garam masala* powder and coriander leaves.

GOBI MUSSALLAM

(Cauliflower roast)

INGREDIENTS

Cauliflower	1 whole
Onions, chopped	2
Tomatoes, chopped	2
Ginger, chopped	1
Salt	to taste
Chilli powder	1 tsp
Coriander powder	1 tsp
Dry mango powder (*amchur*)	½ tsp
Garam masala	½ tsp
Oil	2 tbsp
Peas, boiled	½ cup
Sugar	½ tsp

METHOD

1. Pressure-cook the whole cauliflower completely with a little water and salt (just one whistle will be enough). Keep aside.

2. Heat oil in a pan and fry the onions till golden brown.

3. Add tomatoes and ginger. Fry till oil separates from the mixture.

4. Add all the spices and fry again for sometime.

5. Place the cauliflower on a serving dish. With the help of a knife, stuff the masala inside the cauliflower.

6. Pour the rest of the masala on top. Cook in a microwave oven for two mins.

7. Garnish with peas and serve.

KANDAHARI NAAN

(*Fluffy bread from the North-West Frontier*)

INGREDIENTS

FOR DOUGH:

Refined flour/*maida*	3 cups
Curd	½ cup
Butter	4 tsp
Sugar	½ tsp
Baking powder	1 tsp
Soda powder	1 tsp
Clarified butter/*ghee*	2-4 tsp
Salt	to taste
Eggs (optional)	2

FOR TOPPING:

Tomato sauce	4 tbsp
Honey	1 tsp
Red chilli powder	1 tsp
Salt	to taste
Assorted nuts	½ cup

Mix all the ingredients for topping and keep aside.

METHOD

1. Make a dough mixing all the ingredients. Keep aside for 2-3 hours.

2. Divide the dough into 7-8 balls. Roll out each ball with the help of a rolling pin.

3. Smear the tops with *ghee* and spread the topping on each.

4. Grill in a preheated *tandoor* or oven till the breads turn golden brown.

5. Serve hot as an accompaniment with *dal makhani*.

HANDI BIRYANI

INGREDIENTS

Rice, boiled	2 cups
Onions, chopped	2 medium-sized
Ginger, chopped	2 tbsp
Tomatoes (chopped)	2
Cauliflower, (cut into big florets), carrot, peas and beans	1½ cups, altogether
Milk	2 tbsp
Saffron (*kesar*)	a few leaves
Cardamom	2-3
Cumin seeds	½ tsp
Garam masala powder	½ tsp
Oil	2 tbsp
Onions for garnish, sliced and fried till brown	2
Clarified butter/*Ghee*	1 tbsp

METHOD

1. Heat oil in a pan. Fry ginger and onions till golden brown. Add tomatoes and fry for sometime.
2. Add salt, red chilli and *garam masala* powders and fry.
3. Soak the saffron in milk and keep aside.
4. Crush the cardamom to a powder.
5. In a metal or clay pot (*handi*) or a heat-proof serving dish, cook all the vegetables along with the fried spices and a little water till half-done.
6. Put one layer of the vegetables on the *handi* and place a layer of rice on top of that. Pour the saffron and cardamom powder and repeat the same process. On the final layer of rice, sprinkle fried onions and smear with *ghee*.
7. Cover the *handi* with a lid and seal with wheatflour or refined flour dough tightly.
8. Leave on slow fire for 10 minutes and serve hot in the same *handi*.

BHURANI

INGREDIENTS

Curd	2 cups
Garlic	4 cloves
Salt, black pepper, red chilli and roasted cumin seed powder	to taste

METHOD

1. Keep curd on a strainer for half-an-hour.
2. Grind the garlic to a paste.
3. Mix all the ingredients, put in two cubes of ice and serve.

Bundi Ladoo

INGREDIENTS

Sugar	3 cups
Water	1 cup
Milk	tbsp
Saffron strands	a few
Gramflour	1½ cup
Salt	a pinch
Soda bi-carbonate	2 pinches
Oil	for deep-frying
Melted clarified butter/*ghee*	1 tbsp
Almonds, blanched and sliced	4
Pistachio nuts, blanched and sliced	4
Green cardamoms, crushed	4

FOR DECORATION

Edible silver foil, *(varak)* optional	a few

METHOD

1. Mix sugar with ¼ the water in a saucepan and put to boil. Add the milk.

2. Boil the syrup steadily until it reaches the soft stage (135-145 C/270-290 F) on a sugar thermometer. At this stage, a few drops of syrup dropped into cold water should form threads, which are hard but not brittle.

3. Place the saffron in a small basin with a little water. Place the basin in a saucepan of hot water and rub the saffron occasionally until the strands dissolve.

4. Add the saffron liquid to the syrup, set aside and keep warm.

5. Mix the gramflour, salt and bicarbonate of soda. Add the remaining water to make a thick batter.

6. Heat the oil for deep-frying.

7. Drop small, even portions of the batter off a spoon into the hot oil and fry until golden brown. The cooked *bundis* should be about the size of large peas. Drain on absorbent kitchen paper.

8. Soak the *bundis* in the syrup and leave to stand for 10 minutes. Add melted *ghee*, almonds, pistachios and cardamoms to the *bundis* and mix well.

9. Using a wet metal spoon, shape the *bundis* into small balls and place on a serving platter. Decorate with edible silver foil and serve.

Tomato Shorba
Chana Chaat
Kadhi Pakora
Palak Paneer
Jeera Pullao
Mixed Raita
Methi Roti
Malpuda

TOMATO SHORBA

(Tomato soup)

INGREDIENTS

Tomatoes, ripe	½ kg
Onion, chopped	½
Bay leaf	1
Cinnamon	1 stick
Salt	to taste
Red chilli powder	a pinch
Ginger	½ tsp
Coriander leaves	few

METHOD

1. Mix all the ingredients except coriander leaves.
2. Boil with 3 cups of water.
3. Mash and strain.
4. Garnish with coriander leaves and serve.

CHANA CHAAT

(Spicy chickpeas)

INGREDIENTS

White chickpeas (*chana*)	1 cup
Onion, finely chopped	1
Tomato, finely chopped	1
Cucumber, finely chopped	½
Coriander leaves, chopped	few
Green chillies, chopped	2
Salt	to taste
Chaat masala	½ tsp
Lime juice	1 tbsp
Chilli powder	¼ tsp
Green or raw mango chopped (optional),	½

METHOD

1. Soak the *chana* overnight.
2. Pressure-cook the *chana* with a little salt and chill in the freezer.
3. Mix all the ingredients with *chana* except coriander leaves.
4. Garnish with coriander leaves and serve.

KADHI PAKORA

(Gramflour fritters in yogurt)

INGREDIENTS

FOR CURRY:

Curd	2 cups
Gramflour	2-3 tbsp
Curry leaves	few
Salt	to taste
Turmeric powder	½ tsp
Fenugreek seeds	1½ tsp
Mustard seeds	1½ tsp
Carom seeds	1½ tsp
Asafoetida (*hing*)	a pinch

FOR PAKORAS

Gramflour	3 tbsp
Red chilli powder	½ tsp
Salt	to taste
Soda bi-carbonate	a pinch
Oil	for deep-frying

FOR SEASONING

Oil	2 tbsp
Whole red chillies	2-3
Red chilli powder	1 tsp

METHOD

FOR CURRY:

1. Beat the curd very well, after adding gramflour.
2. Heat 2 tsp oil and add asafoetida, mustard, fenugreek and carom seeds.
3. When they start to crackle, add curry leaves.
4. Now add the beaten curd mixed with gramflour.
5. Add 2-3 cups of water and keep stirring till it boils.
6. Let the curry boil for half-an-hour.

FOR PAKORAS:

1. Mix gramflour, salt, red chilli powder and soda powder with a little water.
2. Keep this batter aside for 5-10 minutes.
3. Heat oil and fry lemon-sized balls of the batter by dropping them in oil with a spoon.
4. Fry the *pakoras* on slow flame till golden brown.
5. Remove the *pakoras* and soak in water.
6. Squeeze out water from the *pakoras* and immerse in the curry.
7. Boil and cook for 5 minutes.
8. Pour into a serving dish.
9. Heat oil for seasoning and fry whole red chillies and chilli powder.
10. Garnish the curry with this seasoning and serve hot.

PALAK PANEER

(Cottage cheese in creamy spinach gravy)

INGREDIENT

Spinach, chopped	2 cups
Cottage cheese/*paneer,* cut into cubes	½ cup
Onion, grated	1, big
Ginger paste	1 tsp
Garlic paste	1 tsp
Tomato puree	from 1 big-sized tomato
Salt	to taste
Red chilli powder	¼ tsp
Dry mango powder (*amchur*)	½ tsp
Garam masala powder	½ tsp
Coriander powder	1 tsp
Oil	2 tsp
Fresh cream/white butter	1 tbsp (optional)

METHOD

1. Heat oil in a pan, add grated onion, ginger and garlic pastes and fry till onion becomes light brown in colour.

2. Add tomato puree and fry for 4-5 minutes.

3. Boil the spinach and grind to a paste.

4. Add all the spices to onion and tomato puree.

5. Fry for sometime. Add spinach paste and cottage cheese cubes.

6. Keep on fire for 10 minutes. If required, add a little water.

7. Garnish with fresh cream or white butter and serve hot.

JEERA PULLAO

(Cumin flavoured pilaff)

INGREDIENTS

Rice	1 cup
Cumin seeds	1 tsp
Bay leaves	2
Cinnamon	2 sticks
Cloves	1-2
Oil	2 tbsp
Onion, sliced and fried golden brown	1
Garam masala powder	1 tsp

METHOD

1. Wash the rice and soak for 10-15 minutes.

2. Heat oil in a pan, add cumin seeds, cinnamon and cloves.

3. Add the rice, 2 cups of water, salt and *garam masala* powder.

4. Stir and cover the pan with a lid.

5. When rice is fully cooked, put on a serving dish, garnish with onion slices and serve hot.

MIXED RAITA

INGREDIENTS

Curd	2 cups
Tomato, chopped finely	¼ of a medium-sized tomato
Onion, chopped finely	¼ of a small onion
Cucumber, chopped finely	¼
Salt	to taste
Roasted cumin seed powder	½ tsp
Red chilli powder	½ tsp
Sugar	a pinch

METHOD

1. Beat the curd well.
2. Mix all the ingredients and chill in the refrigerator.
3. Serve cold.

METHI ROTI

(Fenugreek-flavoured wholewheat bread)

INGREDIENTS

Wheatflour (*atta*)	1 cup
Gramflour	1 cup
Fenugreek leaves, chopped	½ cup
Salt	to taste
Red chilli powder	½ tsp
Dry mango powder (*amchur*)	½ tsp
Garam masala powder	½ tsp
Oil	1 tbsp
Clarified butter ghee	for garnish

METHOD

1. Mix all the ingredients and add sufficient quantity of water to make a dough.
2. Keep aside for 10 minutes.

3. Roll out *chapatis* from the dough and cook on hot griddle or *tandoor*/grill. When they turn golden brown, smear with *ghee* or butter and serve.

MALPUDA

INGREDIENTS

FOR BATTER:

Refined flour	1¾ cup
Baking powder	1½ tsp
Yogurt	¾ cup
Milk	¾ cup
Oil	for deep-frying

FOR SYRUP:

Sugar	1 cup
Saffron (*kesar*)	a few strands
Lime juice	1 tsp
Water	2 cups

METHOD

1. Sieve together the flour and baking powder. Mix in the yogurt and add enough milk to make a thick batter.
2. Boil the sugar, water, lime juice and make sugar syrup by keeping on fire for 10 minutes; add saffron.
3. Heat oil in a wok over medium-high heat. Drop in 1 tbsp of the batter at a time and fry until crisp and brown. Drain on paper towels.
4. Soak the fried *malpudas* in sugar syrup for 5 minutes. Serve with a little syrup on top, hot or cold.

CONTEMPORARY MENUS

1 MENU

Pea Soup
Sweet Lime Salad
Split Red Gram with Drumsticks
Kadak Bhindi
Potato Raita
Tandoori Roti
Steamed Rice
Fresh Tropical Fruits with Vanilla Ice Cream

PEA SOUP

INGREDIENTS

Peas, shelled	125 gm/1¼ cup
Carrot, chopped	1, small
Onion, sliced	¼
Salt, pepper	to taste
Cinnamon stick	½ taste
Clove	1
Bay leaf	1
Butter	½ tsp
Cornflour	½ tsp
Milk	6 tbsp
Bread croutons	few

METHOD

1. Boil peas, carrots, onion and whole spices.
2. When tender, wash and strain.
3. Prepare white sauce with butter, cornflour and milk, as explained in the Basic Recipes section.
4. Add the strained vegetable puree to the sauce.
5. Add salt and pepper and serve hot.

SWEET LIME SALAD

INGREDIENTS

Lettuce leaves	5-6
Watermelon, cut into marble-sized round pieces	8 pieces
Sweet lime (*mausambi*), skinned and cut lengthwise	½
Carrot, cut into thin matchstick pieces	1 large
Cucumber, cut into thin matchstick pieces	½

FOR THE DRESSING:

Tomatoes, boiled, peeled and finely crushed	2
Salad oil or olive oil	1 tbsp
Mustard seeds	½ tsp
Whole red chillies	2-3
Sugar	a pinch
Salt	to taste
Curry leaves	few sprigs

METHOD

1. Heat oil in a pan. Add mustard seeds. Wait till they start to crackle and add curry leaves. Break open the red chillies and release into the pan.
2. Now add tomato puree, salt and sugar. Keep on slow fire for 5 minutes.
3. Arrange the lettuce leaves on a serving dish. Place the cucumber and carrot sticks at the centre, making a circle. Around the circle, arrange watermelon balls and sweet lime.
4. Pour the dressing along the sides of the dish, around the fruits.
5. Serve immediately.

SPLIT RED GRAM WITH DRUMSTICKS

INGREDIENTS

Split red gram (*arhar dal*)	1 cup
Salt	to taste
Turmeric powder	½ tsp
Curry leaves	few
Onions, chopped	2
Tomatoes, chopped	2
Whole red chillies	2-3
Mustard seeds	½ tsp
Green chillies, chopped	2-3
Lime juice	2 tbsp
Red chilli powder	½ tsp
Drumsticks	4
Oil	2 tbsp

METHOD

1. Boil the *dal* with salt, turmeric powder and a few curry leaves.

2. Now cut the drumsticks lengthwise in 2" pieces. Mix them in the *dal* and boil till soft. Keep aside.

3. Heat oil in a pan and add mustard seeds and curry leaves.

4. When the mustard seeds start to crackle, add whole red chillies and onions. Fry the onions till golden brown and then add tomatoes.

5. When tomatoes are soft and the oil separates from the *masala,* add red chilli powder. Fry for sometime and add the *dal* with drumsticks, green chillies, and lime juice.

6. Boil and cook for 5-7 minutes. Add some water if required and serve.

KADAK BHINDI

(*Crunchy okra*)

INGREDIENTS

Ladys' finger/Okra, cut	3 cups
Cumin seeds	½ tsp
Salt	to taste
Asafoetida (*hing*)	a pinch
Red chilli powder	½ tsp
Coriander powder	1 tsp
Garam masala powder	½ tsp
Oil	3 tbsp
Dry mango powder (*amchur*)	¾ tsp

METHOD

1. Cut the okra into small pieces.

2. Heat oil in a wok. Add asafoetida and cumin seeds.

3. When they start to brown, add the okra.

4. Keep stirring on slow fire.

5. Cook till the okra becomes light black and crisp.

6. Add all the spices and serve.

POTATO RAITA

INGREDIENTS

Curd	2 cups
Potatoes	2 small
Black pepper powder	1 tsp
Roasted cumin seed powder	½ tsp
Red chilli powder	½ tsp
Sugar	a pinch
Salt	to taste

METHOD

1. Boil the potatoes.

2. Peel them and chop into small pieces.

3. Beat the curd and add the chopped potatoes to it.

4. Mix in salt, black pepper powder and sugar.

5. Sprinkle some more black pepper powder and cumin seed powder and serve.

TANDOORI ROTI

INGREDIENTS

Wheatflour (*atta*)	2 cups
Salt	½ tsp
Water	to make the dough
Oil	1 tsp

METHOD

1. Add enough water to the wheatflour and make a dough by adding salt and oil. Keep aside for 10-15 minutes.

2. Divide the dough in 4-5 parts, roll out *chapatis* with a rolling pin and put them in a heated gas *tandoor* (oven).

3. When they turn golden brown, serve with a little butter, *ghee* or plain, as desired, as an accompaniment with crunchy okra.

STEAMED RICE

INGREDIENTS

Rice	1 cup
Lime juice	1 tsp
Water	3-4 cups

METHOD

1. Soak the rice in water for 10-15 minutes.

2. Boil water and add rice. Stir every 2 minutes. When it is half-cooked, add some lime juice.

3. After the rice is fully cooked, put it on the strainer for 10-15 minutes.

4. Let the extra water drain out. Serve hot.

Fresh Tropical Fruits with Vanilla Ice Cream

INGREDIENTS

Apple, peeled and cut into cubes	**1**
Bananas, peeled and cut into big pieces	**2 small**
Mango, peeled and cut into small pieces	**1**
Leechis, shelled and broken into pieces	**a few**
Oranges, deseeded, skinned and peeled	**2**
Cherries	**a few**
Grapes	**1 cup without seeds**
Pomegranates, deseeded	**½ cup**
Vanilla ice cream	**½ of a big brick or 1 small brick**
Castor sugar	**2 tbsp**
Lime juice	**1 tsp**

METHOD

1. Melt the vanilla ice cream by beating with a spoon.

2. Cut all the fruits and mix with sugar and lime juice. Chill in the refrigerator for ½ an hour.

3. Mix fruits with vanilla ice cream. Pour into a square serving basin and refrigerate for 1 hour.

4. Serve immediately. (You can garnish with chocolate sauce, jujubes or chocolate chips).

Note: You can add any other seasonal fruit you like to this dessert.

2

Mixed Vegetable Soup
Sprout Salad
Papad Curry
Plain Khichdi
Dry Karela
Plain Khichdi
Alu Parantha
Pudeena Raita
Jehangiri Jalebi

MIXED VEGETABLE SOUP

INGREDIENTS

Spinach	a few leaves
Tomato	1
Beans	a few
Peas	½ cup
Carrot	1
Cauliflower	½ cup
Bottle gourd (*lauki*)	½ cup
Lime juice	to taste
Salt	to taste
Pepper	to taste
Lemon slices	a few

METHOD

1. Mix all the ingredients except the lemon slices with 2 cups of water and boil.
2. Blend in a mixer and strain.
3. Serve with lemon slices.

SPROUT SALAD

INGREDIENTS

Sprouted green gram (*moong*)	1 cup (boiled)
Lettuce leaves	a few
Onion, sliced	1
Tomato, sliced	1
Baby corn, boiled	5-6 pieces

FOR DRESSING:

Vinegar	2 tbsp
Salt	to taste
Freshly crushed black pepper	½ tsp
Sugar	a pinch
Mustard powder	a pinch

METHOD

1. Mix the ingredients for salad in a mixing bowl.
2. Mix the ingredients for dressing.
3. Pour the dressing on the salad and mix well.
4. Chill for 5 minutes and serve.

Papad Curry

INGREDIENTS

Curd	2 cups
Gramflour	1 tsp
Salt	to taste
Turmeric powder	½ tsp
Cumin seeds	½ tsp
Asafoetida (*hing*)	a pinch
Papad, broken into small pieces	2-3
Red chilli powder	½ tsp
Garam masala powder	½ tsp
Oil	2 tbsp

METHOD

1. Beat the curd with gramflour and 1 cup of water.
2. Heat oil in a pan and add asafoetida and cumin seeds. When they turn brown, add red chilli powder.
3. Add the beaten curd to the pan. Stir constantly till it boils.
4. When it is fully boiled, add salt, turmeric powder and the *papad* pieces. Keep stirring on slow fire.
5. Bring to a boil and cook for 5 minutes. Add *garam masala* powder and serve hot.

Dry Karela

(*Dry bitter gourd*)

INGREDIENTS

Bitter gourd/*karela,* chopped	4
Onion, chopped	1
Green chillies, chopped	2
Salt	to taste
Turmeric powder	½ tsp
Coriander powder	1 tsp
Red chilli powder	½ tsp
Dry mango powder (*amchur*)	½ tsp
Garam masala powder	½ tsp
Mustard oil/refined oil	2 tbsp
Cumin seeds	½ tsp
Thread	for tying
Aniseed (*saunf*)	½ tsp

METHOD

1. Wash and peel the *karelas*. Slit from one side and remove the pulp inside. Apply salt on the pieces and also some on the peels and the pulp. Keep aside for 1-2 hours.
2. Wash the *karela* pieces and the peels to remove extra salt and bitterness.
3. Heat oil in a pan, add onion pieces and fry till golden brown. Add the *karela* peels and pulp. Add all the spices and cover and cook for 10-15 minutes.
4. Stuff this filling in all the *karela* pieces kept aside earlier and tie them with thread.
5. Heat 2 tbsp of oil in a pan and add cumin seeds. Fry the *karelas* in this till they become golden brown and crispy. Now turn the other side and fry.
6. Remove the threads and serve hot.

PLAIN KHICHDI

(Rice gruel)

INGREDIENTS

Rice	1 cup
Split green gram (*moong dal*)	½ cup
Salt	to taste
Turmeric powder	½ tsp
Ginger, chopped	1 tsp
Clarified butter or *ghee*	2 tbsp

METHOD

1. Wash the rice and *dal* and soak together for ½ an hour.
2. Add all the ingredients to the rice/*dal* mixture (except *ghee*) and cook in a pressure cooker with 4 cups of water for 10-15 minutes on slow fire.
3. Garnish with *ghee* and serve hot.

ALU PARANTHA

(Parantha stuffed with potatoes)

INGREDIENTS

Wheatflour (*atta*)	2 cups
Salt	to taste
Water	1 cup (for kneading the dough)

FOR FILLING:

Potatoes, boiled, peeled and mashed	2
Salt	to taste
Green chilli, finely chopped	1
Dry mango powder (*amchur*)	½ tsp
Garam masala powder	½ tsp
Coriander leaves	few chopped
Ghee/oil	4 tbsp

METHOD

1. Make a dough by mixing wheatflour, salt and water. Keep aside for 10-15 minutes.
2. Mix all the ingredients for filling.
3. Divide the dough in four portions. With a rolling pin, roll one part into a circular and thick *parantha*.
4. Apply a little oil and put in some filling. Close and roll it again with the help of dry flour. Repeat for the other portions of the dough.
5. Heat the *paranthas* from both sides on a hot griddle, smearing the sides with oil. Cook till they are golden brown from both sides.
6. Serve hot with chilli pickle.

PUDEENA RAITA

(Mint raita)

INGREDIENTS

Curd	2 cups
Mint leaves (*pudina*), finely crushed	few
Salt	to taste
Roasted cumin seed powder	½ tsp
Red chilli powder	½ tsp
Sugar	a pinch

METHOD

1. Beat the curd well.
2. Mix all the ingredients and chill in the refrigerator.
3. Serve cold.

JEHANGIRI JALEBI

INGREDIENTS

Refined flour (*maida*)	1 cup
Curd	¼ cup
Water	3½ cups
Sugar	3 cups
Saffron or rose water	a pinch
Artificial yellow colour (available in the market)	a few drops
Cardamom powder	½ tsp
Oil	for deep-frying

FOR DECORATION

Edible silver foil, (*varak*) optional	a few

METHOD

1. Mix flour, curd and water to a smooth creamy consistency and leave overnight, or for 15 hours, to ferment. Mix saffron in the batter.
2. Make a thick sugar syrup with 3 cups of water, add crushed saffron and yellow colour. If you use rose water instead of saffron, let the syrup cool slightly before adding it. Add cardamom powder.
3. Use an icing gun with a ¼" plain nozzle and fill with some of the fermented flour batter. Squeeze the batter in circles over oil, making little rings all around each basic circle.
4. Deep-fry on both sides till the *jalebis* become crisp and golden. Take each out carefully, drain excess oil and put into warm syrup.
5. Remove after two minutes and drain well. Repeat for the rest of the batter.
6. Arrange the *Jehangiri Jalebis* on a flat serving dish. Garnish with silver *varak* and serve.

Tomato Soup with Vegetables
Spicy Lettuce Salad
Dal Palak
Stuffed Tomatoes
Sweet Rice
Pineapple Raita
Phulka/Chapati
Gajar Kheer

TOMATO SOUP WITH VEGETABLES

INGREDIENTS

Tomatoes	5 big/500 gm
Carrot, peas, beans, cauliflower, chopped and boiled	1 cup
Salt	to taste
Black pepper	to taste
Onion, chopped	½ tsp
Ginger, chopped	½ tsp
Garlic, chopped	½ tsp

METHOD

1. Boil the tomatoes with salt, onion, ginger, garlic and 3 cups of water.
2. Blend and strain.
3. Mix all the vegetables, salt, black pepper and serve hot.

SPICY LETTUCE SALAD

INGREDIENTS

Green lettuce	7-8 leaves
Red lettuce	7-8 leaves
Carrot	1
Tomato	1
Red capsicum	½

DRESSING:

Vinegar	3 tbsp
Red Tabasco	1 tbsp

OR

Capsico sauce	1 tbsp
Salt	to taste
Sugar	½ tsp

METHOD

1. Wash and keep the lettuce in chilled water with a pinch of salt.
2. Cut carrots and capsicum into matchstick-sized pieces.
3. Deseed the tomato and cut thinly lengthwise.
4. In a mixing bowl, break salad leaves into two pieces each and put all other vegetables.
5. Mix the ingredients for the dressing and pour on the salad.
6. Mix the dressing and salad together and serve.

DAL PALAK

(Spinach with lentil)

INGREDIENTS

Split green gram (*moong dal*)	½ cup
Spinach, chopped	3 cups
Salt	to taste
Red chilli powder	½ tsp
Cumin seeds	¼ tsp
Curd	1 cup
Asafoetida (hing)	a pinch
Turmeric powder	½ tsp
Oil	2 tbsp

METHOD

1. Pressure-cook the *dal*, spinach, salt and turmeric powder with 2 cups of water.
2. Beat the *dal* nicely and add beaten curd, while *dal* boils.
3. Cook for 4-5 minutes.
4. Pour *dal* into a serving dish. Heat oil in a pan, add asafoetida and cumin seeds. When they turn brown, add chilli powder and pour on the *dal*. Serve hot.

STUFFED TOMATOES

INGREDIENTS

Ripe tomatoes	4
Cottage cheese/*paneer*	1 cup
Onion, chopped	1
Green chillies, chopped	1
Salt	to taste
Red chilli powder	¼ tsp
Dry mango powder (*amchur*)	½ tsp
Garam masala powder	½ tsp
Fresh coriander leaves	a sprig

METHOD

1. Cut the top portions of tomatoes and keep them aside. Scoop out the pulp from inside.
2. Mix mashed *paneer*, onion, green chilli, salt, red chilli, *amchur* and *garam masala* powders.
3. Fill all the scooped tomatoes with this *paneer* mixture. Close the tomatoes with the sliced top portions and pierce with a toothpick from the top so that the filling does not come out.
4. Heat oil in a pan and shallow fry the tomatoes on slow fire for 10-15 minutes, without covering the pan.
5. When tomatoes are cooked, put them on a serving dish.
6. Heat the tomato pulp with salt, black pepper and a pinch of sugar.
7. Pour this on the stuffed tomatoes.
8. Remove the tooth picks, garnish with coriander leaves and serve hot.

SWEET RICE

INGREDIENTS

Boiled rice	2 cups
Sugar	4 tsp
Saffron (*kesar*)	few strands
Milk	2 tbsp
Almonds, crushed	2 tbsp
Cardamom seeds/syrup	2 seeds/few drops
Raisins	2 tbsp
Clarified butter/*Ghee*	1 tbsp

METHOD

1. Soak the saffron in milk for 10-15 minutes.
2. Add sugar, rice and milk to it.
3. Heat *ghee* in a pan, add almonds, raisins and rice-mixture. Finally pour the cardamom syrup.
4. Keep stirring till the sugar melts.
5. Serve hot.

PINEAPPLE RAITA

INGREDIENTS

Curd	2 cups
Pineapple chunks	2 tbsp
Sugar	1½ tsp

METHOD

Mix all the ingredients. Chill and serve.

PHULKA/CHAPATI

(*Wheatflour bread*)

INGREDIENTS

Wheatflour (*atta*)	2 cups
Salt	½ tsp
Water	to make the dough
Clarified butter/*ghee*	2 tbsp

METHOD

1. Add sufficient water to the wheatflour to make the dough and keep aside for 10-15 minutes.
2. Divide the dough into small ball-sized portions.

3. Using dry flour and a rolling pin roll out one portion and place it on a hot griddle. After 2 minutes turn the other side.
4. Roast the *chapati* directly on fire by holding with a pair of aluminum tongs till golden brown from both the sides. Repeat for all portions of the dough.
5. Apply *ghee* on the *chapatis* and serve hot.

GAJAR KHEER

(*Carrot pudding*)

INGREDIENTS

Milk	4 cups
Carrots	4
Sugar	6 tbsp
Nuts	a few

METHOD

1. Grate carrots finely.
2. Boil milk, add carrot and cook on slow fire till milk thickens.
3. Add sugar, cook for a minute, and remove from fire.
4. Serve hot or cold garnished with chopped nuts.

MENU

4

Green Pea-Skin Soup
Beetroot Salad
Alu Gravy
Masala Bhindi
Raw Mango Panna
Dal Puri/Kachori
Suji Halwa

GREEN PEA-SKIN SOUP

INGREDIENTS

Skin of green peas	4 cups
Green peas, blanched	1 cup
Onion, chopped	1
Milk	3 cups
Butter	2 tsp
Salt and pepper	to taste
Lime slice	1

METHOD

1. Heat butter and fry chopped onion slices for 1 minute.
2. Add the pea-skins and half the peas and cook for 3-4 minutes.
3. Add milk and ½ cup water and pressure-cook till soft.
4. Blend in a mixer and strain.
5. Boil the stock and cook for 1 minute. Separately, boil the rest of the blanched peas with a little salt.
6. Add this to the stock along with salt and pepper.
7. Serve hot with lime slice.

BEETROOT SALAD

INGREDIENTS

Beetroot, boiled, peeled and cut into cubes	3
Salt	to taste
Pepper	1 tsp
Lime juice	2 tsp
Lettuce leaves	a few
Tomato, cut into cubes	1
Spring onions, cut like rings	3
Coriander leaves, chopped	a few

METHOD

1. Chill the beetroot in the refrigerator.
2. Place salad leaves on a serving dish. Mix beetroot, salt, pepper, lime juice and tomatoes and put on top of lettuce leaves.
3. Garnish with spring onions and coriander leaves and serve.

ALU GRAVY

(Potato curry)

INGREDIENTS

Potatoes, boiled, peeled and cut into small pieces	4
Tomatoes, boiled, peeled and chopped	4
Oil	3 tbsp
Cumin seeds	½ tbsp
Bay leaves	2
Ginger, chopped	1 tsp
Green chillies, chopped	2-3
Salt	to taste
Coriander powder	2 tsp
Red chilli powder	¾ tsp
Garam masala powder	½ tsp
Turmeric powder	½ tsp
Dry mango powder (*amchur*)	½ tsp
Dry fenugreek leaves (*kasoori methi*)	½ tsp

METHOD

1. Heat oil in a pan. Fry cumin seeds and bay leaves. Add tomatoes, ginger and green chillies. Fry till tomatoes are soft.
2. Add the *methi* or fenugreek leaves along with all the spices except *amchur* powder.
3. Fry for 3 minutes and add potatoes with 2 cups of water. Boil and cook for 10-15 minutes.
4. Add *amchur* powder and serve hot.

MASALA BHINDI

(Spicy okra)

INGREDIENTS

Lady's finger/okra, washed and cut into ½" pieces	2 cups
Onions, chopped	2
Ginger, chopped	1 tsp
Salt	to taste
Coriander powder	2 tsp
Turmeric powder	½ tsp
Garam masala powder	½ tsp
Red chilli powder	½ tsp
Dry mango powder (*amchur*)	½ tsp
Cumin seeds	½ tsp
Tomato, sliced into cubes	1
Oil	2 tbsp

METHOD

1. Heat oil in a pan, add cumin seeds. After 1 minute, add onions and ginger. Fry till onions are soft.
2. Add okra and fry on slow fire, stirring constantly, till they become soft and crispy. Add all the spices. Mix well, leave on fire for 2-3 minutes.
3. Garnish with tomatoes and serve hot.

RAW MANGO PANNA

(Tangy raw mango sherbet)

INGREDIENTS

Raw mangoes	2
Sugar	4 tbsp
Salt	to taste
Roasted cumin seeds, powdered	1½ tsp

Red chilli powder	1½ tsp
Fresh mint leaves	made into paste
Ice cubes	a few

METHOD

1. Boil the mangoes, make a puree and strain.
2. Add all the spices, mix well, add ice cubes and 1 cup of water.
3. Serve chilled.

DAL PURI/KACHORI

(Deep-fried wholewheat bread stuffed with Bengal gram)

INGREDIENTS

FOR DOUGH:

Wheatflour (*atta*)	2 cups
Salt	to taste
Melted fat	1 tsp

FOR STUFFING:

Bengal gram (*chana dal*)	2 tbsp
Ginger	a small piece
Green chilli	½
Cumin seeds	1/8 tsp
Dry mango powder (*amchur*)	a pinch
Red chilli powder	a pinch
Garam masala powder	a pinch
Soda	a pinch
Oil	for frying

METHOD

1. Soak *dal* overnight, drain and grind to a coarse paste without adding water. Add chopped ginger, green chilli and soda and mix well.

2. Sift the wheatflour and add salt and rub in the melted fat.
3. Make a soft dough using water. Leave aside for ½ an hour.
4. Knead the dough again using a little oil.
5. Divide into 4 portions and shape into balls.
6. Make a depression in the centre of a ball and fill with the *dal* mixture and again shape it into a ball. Repeat for the rest of the dough.
7. Roll the balls into flat round circles, using oil.
8. Deep dry from both sides.
9. Serve as an accompaniment.

SUJI HALWA

(Semolina dessert)

INGREDIENTS

Fine semolina	1 cup
Almonds, chopped	2 tbsp
Sugar	½ cup
Clarified butter/*ghee*	2 tbsp
Water	3 cups

METHOD

1. Heat *ghee* in a wok; add chopped nuts, fry for 1 minute. Add the semolina and keep stirring till it becomes golden brown.
2. Separately, heat 3 cups of water.
3. With one hand continue to stir and with the other, pour water into the semolina slowly. Keep stirring till it becomes a little thick.
4. Add sugar and serve hot.

5

MENU

Tomato Soup
Moth Chaat
Moong Wadi with Papad
Achaari Gobi
Lauki Raita
Chickmari Rice
Spicy Masala Roti
Almond Ice Sundae

TOMATO SOUP

INGREDIENTS

Tomatoes	½ kg
Potatoes	1
Milk	½ cup
Salt	to taste
Black pepper	to taste
Sugar	2 tsp
Bread	2 slices
Oil	for frying

METHOD

1. Boil the tomatoes and potatoes with salt and 1 cup of water.
2. Mix in the blender and strain.
3. Add salt and pepper.
4. While the soup is on the fire, keep adding milk, stirring continuously.
5. Cut bread into small cubes and deep fry till golden brown.
6. Serve hot soup with bread croutons.

MOTH CHAAT

INGREDIENTS

Brown whole pulses (*moth dal*)	1 cup
Onion, chopped	1
Tomato, chopped	1
Cucumber, chopped	½
Green chillies, chopped	2
Salt	to taste
Lime juice	1 tsp
Red chilli powder	¼ tsp
Chaat masala	½ tsp
Coriander leaves	a few

METHOD

1. Soak the *moth* pulses overnight. Remove extra water and put on a wet cloth, cover and keep for 24 hours.
2. When they start to sprout, they are ready to use.
3. Boil the *moth* with a little salt and turmeric powder.
4. Mix *moth,* onion, tomato, cucumber, green chillies, salt, lime juice, red chilli powder, *chaat masala* and coriander leaves in a mixing bowl.
5. Chill for 5 minutes and serve.

MOONG VADI WITH PAPAD

(Green gram Vadi with papad)

INGREDIENTS FOR VADI

Washed green gram (*moong dal*), without skin	1 cup
Salt	to taste
Red chilli powder	½ tsp
Garam masala	½ tsp
Cumin seeds	1 tsp
Asafoetida	¼ tsp
Oil	1 tsp

METHOD FOR VADI

1. Soak the *dal* overnight. Drain and blend dry without using water. Make a thick paste.
2. Add all the spices and mix. Place the paste on a plate smeared with oil.
3. Using your hands, make small ball-sized *vadis* (½" in size) out of the paste.
4. Keep under sunlight to dry. When fully dried, store them in an airtight container.

INGREDIENTS FOR MOONG VADI WITH PAPAD CURRY

Vadi, broken into small pieces	½ cup
Papad	3 big-sized
Tomatoes	3
Ginger, chopped	1
Green chillies, chopped	2
Curd	1 cup
Salt	to taste
Red chilli powder	½ tsp
Coriander powder	1½ tsp
Turmeric powder	½ tsp
Garam masala powder	¾ tsp
Oil	3 tbsp
Asafoetida (*hing*)	a pinch
Cumin seeds	½ tsp

METHOD FOR CURRY

1. Heat oil in a pressure cooker and fry asafoetida and cumin seeds.
2. When the cumin seeds become brown, add *moong dal vadis* and fry till golden brown.
3. Add tomatoes, green chillies and ginger and fry till tomatoes are soft and oil separates from the mixture.
4. Add all the spices except *garam masala* powder.
5. Add three to four cups of water and close the lid.
6. Pressure-cook for 10 to 15 minutes.
7. When it is fully cooked, add beaten curd. Keep stirring as you add.
8. Break the *papad* in small pieces (break one *papad* into 6 to 8 pieces) and add to the curry.
9. Boil and cook for 5 minutes. Add water if required.
10. Add *garam masala* powder and serve hot.

ACHAARI GOBI

(Pickle-flavoured cauliflower)

INGREDIENTS

Cauliflower	1 big
Onions, sliced	2
Tomatoes, peeled and sliced	2-3
Red chilli powder	2 tsp
Ginger, chopped	2 tbsp
Garlic, chopped	2 tbsp
Cumin powder	3 tsp
Coriander powder	3 tsp
Juice	of 6 lemons
Green chillies (cut into half)	5
Curry leaves	½ cup
Salt	to taste

FOR *TADKA* OR SEASONING:

Cumin seeds	2 tsp
Nigella seeds (*kalonji*)	½ tsp
Dry whole red chillies	4-5
Mustard seeds	1 tsp
Fenugreek seeds	1 tsp
Oil	½ cup

METHOD

1. Wash and cut the cauliflower in big florets. Steam or parboil them. (Cauliflower should be half-cooked).

2. Heat 2 tbsp oil in a wok and fry onion and curry leaves till onion changes colour.

3. Add ginger and garlic; fry for 4-5 minutes. Add tomatoes.

4. Add cumin powder, coriander powder, chilli powder and fry for a while.

5. Add cauliflower. Cover and cook for 10-15 minutes or till cauliflower is cooked.

6. Heat oil for *tadka*. Fry cumin seeds, *kalonji*, mustard and fenugreek seeds and dry whole red chillies. When all the seeds change colour, pour on the cauliflower.

7. Add lime juice and mix well.

8. Serve hot with *rotis* or bread rolls.

LAUKI RAITA

INGREDIENTS

Curd	2 cups
Bottle gourd/*lauki,* peeled and grated	½ cup
Salt, red chilli powder,	to taste
Roasted and powdered	to taste
Cumin seeds	to taste

METHOD

1. Boil the grated *lauki* in a little water.

2. Beat the curd and add the boiled *lauki* to it.

3. Mix in salt.

4. Sprinkle red chilli and cumin seed powders and serve.

CHICKMARI RICE

(Flavoured rice)

INGREDIENTS

Rice, boiled	2 cups
Cucumber, chopped	½
Ginger, chopped	1 tsp
Mustard seeds	½ tsp
Curry leaves	few
Salt	to taste
Black peppercorns, crushed	¾ tsp
Curd	2 cups
Oil	1 tbsp
Coriander leaves, chopped	1 tbsp

METHOD

1. Heat oil in a pan. Fry mustard seeds and curry leaves.
2. When the mustard seeds start to crackle, add the cucumber and fry till it becomes soft.
3. Add ginger, rice, curd, salt and black pepper. Keep stirring for three to four minutes.
4. Garnish with coriander leaves and serve hot.

SPICY MASALA ROTI

INGREDIENTS

Wheatflour (*atta*)	2 cups
Salt	to taste
Oil	2 tsp
Red chilli powder	1 tsp
Dry mango powder (*amchur*)	1 tsp
Garam masala powder	1 tsp
Clarified butter/*ghee*	2 tbsp

METHOD

1. Make a dough from the wheatflour by adding a little salt, oil and water.
2. Keep aside for 10-15 minutes.
3. Divide the dough into small portions.
4. Roll out the portions into flat circles, apply *ghee*, sprinkle salt, red chilli, *amchur* and *garam masala* powders on each.
5. Close them by folding the corners towards the centre. Now roll once again into flat shapes with the help of dry flour.
6. Roast on a hot griddle till brown and crispy.
7. Apply *ghee* and serve.

ALMOND ICE SUNDAE

INGREDIENTS

Chocolate ice cream	4 scoops
Fresh cream	1 cup
Pineapple chunks	1 small can (500 gm)
Almonds, grated	3 tbsp
Butter	1 tbsp

METHOD

1. Fry almonds in butter till brown and allow to cool.
2. Drain pineapple and arrange on individual dessert dishes.
3. Add a scoop of chocolate ice cream to each dish and decorate with whipped cream.
4. Sprinkle with almonds and serve immediately.

MENU

6

Spinach Soup
Vegetable Sticks with Curd Dip
Masoor Dal Tadka
Stuffed Eggplant/Brinjal
Chutniwale Alu
Pea Pillaf
Laccha Roti
Cottage Cheese and Coconut Balls

SPINACH SOUP

INGREDIENTS

Spinach, chopped	2 cups
Onions, chopped	1 cup
Tomatoes, chopped	1 cup
Skimmed milk	1 cup
Lime slice	1
Cumin seeds	¼ tsp
Oil	¼ tsp
Salt and pepper	¼ tsp

METHOD

1. Boil spinach, onions and tomatoes with salt and 1 cup of water.

2. Blend in the mixer and strain.

3. Put on the fire. Add milk, stirring continuously.

4. Add salt and pepper. Roast cumin seeds separately till brown.

5. Garnish the soup with cumin seeds and serve with lime slice.

VEGETABLE STICKS WITH CURD DIP

INGREDIENTS

Cucumber	1
Carrot	1
Radish	1
Tomato	1
Beetroot	1
Salad leaves	a few

FOR THE DIP:

Curd	3 cups
Onion, chopped	1 small
Tomato sauce	1 tsp
Capsicum, chopped	2 tbsp
Salt	to taste
Black pepper	¼ tsp
Tabasco sauce	1 tsp

METHOD

1. Cut all the vegetables lengthwise.

2. Place the curd in a strainer for ½ an hour.

3. In a bowl mix strained curd, onion, Tabasco, capsicum, salt and black pepper.

4. On a serving dish, arrange the lettuce leaves and all vegetable sticks.

5. Serve with the curd dip.

MASOOR DAL TADKA

(Lentil with spicy seasoning)

INGREDIENTS

De-skinned lentil (*masoor dal*)	1 cup
Onion, chopped	1
Tomatoes, chopped	2
Ginger	1 tbsp
Garlic	1 tbsp
Green chillies	1-2
Curry leaves	few
Salt	to taste
Mustard seeds	½ tsp
Lime juice	2 tbsp
Turmeric powder	½ tsp
Whole red chillies	2-3
Oil	2 tbsp
Coriander leaves, chopped	a few

METHOD

1. Boil the *dal* in 2-3 cups of water, salt and turmeric powder. Keep aside.
2. Heat oil in a pan, add mustard seeds, red chillies and curry leaves.
3. When mustard seeds start to crackle, add onion and fry till golden brown.
4. Add tomatoes, ginger, garlic and green chillies and fry till oil separates.
5. Pour cooked *dal* on the above *masala*.
6. Boil and cook for 5-10 minutes. Add lime juice.
7. Garnish with coriander leaves and serve hot.

STUFFED EGGPLANT/BRINJAL

INGREDIENTS

Eggplant/brinjals	4-5 (small and round)
Salt	¾ tsp
Red chilli powder	½ tsp
Dry mango powder (*amchur*)	½ tsp
Garam masala powder	½ tsp
Coriander powder	1½ tsp
Oil	2 tsp
Cumin seeds	½ tbsp

METHOD

1. Wash and slit two sides of the brinjals, taking care not to cut them fully.
2. Soak the brinjals in water for 2 minutes.
3. Mix all the spices except cumin seeds.
4. Stuff the brinjal pieces with the mixed spices.
5. Heat oil in a wok and add cumin seeds. When they turn brown, add the brinjal pieces and cover the wok.
6. Shallow-fry till brinals are soft and serve hot.

CHUTNIWALE ALU

(Chutneyed potatoes)

INGREDIENTS

Baby potatoes, boiled, de-skinned and chilled	½ kg

FOR CHUTNEY

Coriander leaves	1 bunch
Salt	to taste
Red chilli powder	1-2 tsp
Lime juice	4 tbsp

METHOD

1. Blend all the ingredients for chutney in a blender.
2. Mix potatoes and chutney. Chill and serve.

PEA PILLAF

INGREDIENTS

Rice	1 cup (raw)
Salt	to taste
Cumin seeds	1 tsp
Cinnamon sticks	2
Bay leaves	1-2
Garam masala powder	1 tsp
Peas	½ cup
Oil	2 tsp
Onion, sliced	1

METHOD

1. Clean and wash rice. Soak for 10-15 minutes.
2. Heat oil in a pan. Add bay leaves, cumin seeds and cinnamon.
3. Add peas and rice. Pour two cups of water and add salt and *garam masala* powder.
4. Cover with a lid till the rice is fully cooked.
5. Fry the onion till golden brown, separately.
6. Garnish rice with brown onions and serve hot.
7. Serve with mint raita (recipe given earlier in Contemporary Menu 2).

LACCHA ROTI

INGREDIENTS

Wheatflour (*atta*)	2 cups
Salt	to taste
Oil	2 tbsp

METHOD

1. Make a dough by adding sufficient water and a little salt to the wheatflour. Keep aside for 10-15 minutes.
2. Divide the dough into small portions
3. Roll out each portion with a little dry flour and a rolling pin.
4. Apply oil, roll each portion again from the centre towards the ends, giving it a snake-like shape. Roll once more using dry flour to make flat *rotis*.
5. Roast them in a *tandoor* or oven/grill till both sides are golden brown.
6. Apply butter and serve hot.

COTTAGE CHEESE AND COCONUT BALLS

INGREDIENTS

Cottage cheese/*paneer* 450 gm (grated: 2 cups)	
Icing sugar	**1 cup**
Rose water	**2-3 tsp**
Fresh coconut, finely grated	**½**
Sugar	**½ cup**
Saffron strands	**¼ tsp**
Milk	**1 tsp**
Pistachio nuts, blanched and chopped	**4-5**
Oil	**½ tsp**

FOR DECORATION:

Edible silver foil (*varak*), optional	**a few**

METHOD

1. Grate the *paneer* in a bowl, add icing sugar and rose water. Mix very well to make a dough.

2. Shape spoonfuls of the mixture into small round balls about the size of walnuts.

3. In a saucepan smeared with very little oil, cook coconut and sugar for 10 minutes over low heat, stirring frequently. Cool.

4. Warm the saffron and milk in a small basin placed in saucepan of hot water. Rub the saffron until it dissolves. Add the saffron milk to the coconut and mix well.

5. Coat the *paneer* balls with the coconut mixture, rolling them carefully in the palms of your hands.

6. Arrange the paneer and coconut balls on a serving plate and decorate with silver foil (if you like). Chill thoroughly.

7. To serve, cut each ball into two and decorate with chopped pistachio nuts.

MENU

7

Amras
Moong Dal Shorba
Broccoli, Baby Corn and Mushroom Salad
Plain Kadhi
. Masala Khichdi
Mangoodi Matar
Dry Potato
Plain Puri
Moong Dal Halwa

AMRAS

(Chilled mango sorbet)

INGREDIENTS

Mangoes, ripe	4
Milk	½ cup
Sugar	3 tbsp
Ice cubes	a few

METHOD

1. Squeeze and take out the pulp of the mangoes and strain it.
2. Add milk and sugar to the strained liquid and mix well.
3. Add ice cubes. Chill in the freezer and serve before a meal.

MOONG DAL SHORBA

(Green gram soup)

INGREDIENTS

Green gram (*moong dal*), washed	½ cup
Salt	to taste
Juice	½ lime
Turmeric powder	½ tsp
Cinnamon	1 stick
Cloves	2
Bay leaf	1
Butter	1 tsp
Coriander leaves, chopped	a few

METHOD

1. Wash the *dal* and boil with 2 cups of water, salt, turmeric powder, bay leaf and cinnamon.
2. Blend in a liquidiser.
3. Garnish with butter, lime juice and chopped coriander leaves.
4. Serve hot.

BROCCOLI, BABY CORN AND MUSHROOM SALAD

INGREDIENTS

Baby corn, cut into small pieces	6
Broccoli, cut into small florets	1 small
Mushrooms	½ kg
Onion, sliced	1
Olives, sliced	a few
Thousand Island dressing	4 tbsp

METHOD

1. Parboil/microwave/steam the vegetables. Cool for 15 minutes in the refrigerator.
2. Mix all the vegetables including onion with Thousand Island dressing, garnish with olives and serve chilled.

ALTERNATIVE DRESSING

Vinegar	3-4 tbsp
Olive oil	1 tbsp
Salt	to taste
Black pepper	1 tsp
Mustard powder	½ tsp
Spring onions, chopped	2 tbsp
Tomatoes, chopped	2 tbsp

METHOD

Mix all the ingredients well and add to the salad.

PLAIN KADHI

(Yogurt-flavoured tangy yellow curry)

INGREDIENTS

Curd	2 cups
Gramflour (*besan*)	2 tbsp
Salt	to taste
Turmeric powder	½ tsp
Curry leaves	few
Asafoetida (*hing*)	a pinch
Mustard seeds	½ tsp
Fenugreek seeds	½ tsp
Carom seeds	½ tsp
Garam masala powder	½ tsp
Whole red chillies	2-3
Dry leaves (*kasoori methi*)	1 tbsp femgreek
Oil	2 tbsp

METHOD

1. Beat the curd along with gramflour and 3 cups of water.
2. Heat oil in a pan, add asafoetida, mustard, fenugreek and carom seeds. When they start turning brown, add curry leaves and whole red chillies.
3. Now add the beaten curd to the pan. Keep stirring till it boils. Add dry *methi* leaves and leave on slow fire for half-an-hour. Remove from fire and add *garam masala* powder.

FOR SEASONING:

Oil	2 tbsp
Red chilli powder	1 tsp

Fry red chilli powder in hot oil.
Pour on the *kadhi* and serve hot.

MASALA KHICHDI

(Spicy rice gruel)

INGREDIENTS

Rice	1 cup
Washed green gram (*moong dal*)	¼ cup
Bengal gram (*chana dal*)	¼ cup
Lentil (*masoor dal*)	¼ cup
Mixed vegetables (carrot, peas, cauliflower and beans)	1 cup (cut into big pieces)
Bay leaves	1
Cumin seeds	½ tsp
Oil	2 tbsp
Asafoetida (*hing*)	a pinch
Onion, grated	1
Tomato, grated	1
Salt	to taste
Turmeric powder	½ tsp
Red chilli powder	½ tsp
Garam masala powder	1 tsp
Ginger, grated	1 tsp
Clarified butter (*ghee*)/ butter	1 tbsp

METHOD

1. Wash the *dal* and rice and soak together for 5-10 minutes.
2. Heat oil and add asafoetida, bay leaves and cumin seeds.
3. After one minute, add grated onion and ginger and fry for 5 minutes till they turn brown. Now add the tomato and fry till the oil separates.
4. Add all the spices and fry again for 2 minutes.
5. Add rice and *dal* mixture and water as required (should be about double the quantity of the mixture); pressure-cook for 10 minutes.
6. Top with *ghee* or butter and serve hot.

MANGOODI MATAR

(Green gram vadis with peas)

INGREDIENTS

Green gram (*moong dal*) wadi (*mangoodi*)	½ cup (crushed)
Peas	½ cup
Oil	2 tbsp
Salt	to taste
Turmeric powder	½ tsp
Coriander powder	2 tsp
Red chilli powder	½ tsp
Dry mango powder (*amchur*)	¾ tsp
Garam masala powder	½ tsp
Cumin seeds	½ tsp
Tomatoes, boiled, peeled and chopped	3
Ginger, chopped	1 tbsp
Green chillies, chopped	2
Asafoetida (*hing*)	a pinch

METHOD

1. Heat oil in a pressure cooker, add asafoetida and cumin seeds. After a minute, add the *mangoodis* and fry till they turn light brown.
2. Add chopped tomatoes, ginger and green chillies and fry till tomatoes become soft.
3. Add all the spices except *amchur*. Fry for 2 minutes. Now add peas and 3 cups of water.
4. Pressure-cook for 10 minutes.
5. When soft, add *amchur* powder and serve hot.

DRY POTATO

INGREDIENTS

Potatoes, boiled, peeled and cut into cubes	4, medium-sized
Oil	3 tbsp
Cumin seeds	1 tsp
Salt	to taste
Turmeric powder	½ tsp
Coriander powder	2 tsp
Red chilli powder	¾ tsp
Garam masala powder	1 tsp
Dry mango powder (*amchur*)	1 tsp
Green chillies, chopped	2
Coriander leaves, chopped	few
Lime juice	1 tsp

METHOD

1. Heat oil and add cumin seeds. When they turn brown, add all the spices and green chillies and fry for sometime.
2. Add potatoes. Mix well and cook for 2 minutes.
3. Add lime juice and mix.
4. Garnish with coriander leaves and serve hot.

PLAIN PURI

INGREDIENTS

Wheatflour (*atta*)	2 cups
Oil	1 tsp
Milk	1 cup
Salt	½ tsp
Oil	for deep-frying

METHOD

1. Mix all the ingredients and knead to a hard dough. Keep aside for 10-15 minutes.
2. Divide the dough into 4 small portions.
3. Roll one portion into a 3-4" circular *puri* using some oil. Repeat for the other portions.
4. Fry the *puris* till golden brown from both sides.
5. Serve hot or keep wrapped in silver foil and serve after sometime.

MOONG DAL HALWA

(*Lentil pudding*)

INGREDIENTS

Green gram (*moong dal*)	1 cup
Sugar	½ cup
Clarified butter/*ghee*	1 cup
Milk or water	6 tbsp
Raisins (*kismish*)	few
Saffron	4-5 strands
Mixed nuts (almonds and pistachios), chopped	4 tbsp
Crushed cardamom/ cardamom syrup	½ tsp/a few drops

METHOD

1. Soak *dal* overnight and grind to a paste.
2. Soak, peel and slice the almonds finely.
3. Crush saffron and soak in 1 tbsp of milk.
4. Fry *dal* paste in hot *ghee* till brown, add sugar, nuts, raisins and milk or water.
5. Cook on slow fire, stirring constantly till *ghee* separates from mixture.
6. Add cardamom and saffron. Cook for 5 minutes and serve hot.

8

MENU

Masoor Dal Soup
Baby Corn and Cauliflower Salad
Alu Tamatar
Palak Methi Chaman
Dry Moong Dal
Vegetable Biryani
Plain Raita
Khasta Roti
Rice Kheer

MASOOR DAL SOUP

(*Lentil soup*)

INGREDIENTS

Lentil (*masoor dal*), washed	½ cup
Salt	to taste
Turmeric powder	½ tsp
Onion, sliced	1
Cinnamon	1 stick
Cumin seeds	½ tsp
Fenugreek seeds	½ tsp
Coriander seeds	½ tsp
Aniseed	½ tsp
Ginger, chopped	1 tsp
Rice, boiled	1½ tbsp

METHOD

1. Roast and grind to a powder-coriander seeds, cumin seeds, and aniseed.
2. Boil *dal* with 2 cups of water, salt, turmeric powder, all the spices and ginger.
3. Blend in the mixer.
4. Add boiled rice.
5. Garnish with fried onion slices (optional).

BABY CORN AND CAULIFLOWER SALAD

INGREDIENTS

Baby corn	4-5 pieces
Cauliflower	5 florets
Lettuce	a few leaves
Onion	1, big
Mushrooms	5-6
Tomato	1, big
Roasted sesame seeds	1 tbsp

FOR DRESSING:

Vinegar	2 tbsp
Sugar	½ tsp
Salt	to taste
Black pepper	1 tsp

METHOD

1. Cut cauliflower florets further into medium-sized florets.
2. Cut mushrooms into halves.
3. Parboil the cauliflower, mushroom and baby corn.
4. Chill these vegetables in the refrigerator.
5. Put the lettuce in chilled water and break into small pieces.
6. Mix all the ingredients for dressing very well.
7. Cut tomato and onion lengthwise thinly, like sticks.
8. Mix everything and serve in a salad bowl, garnished with sesame seeds.

ALU TAMATAR

(Tomato flavoured potato curry)

INGREDIENTS

Potatoes, peeled and cut into small pieces	2, big
Tomatoes, boiled and peeled	4, medium
Ginger, chopped	1 tsp
Green chillies, chopped	1-2
Coriander leaves, chopped	a few
Salt	to taste
Cumin seeds	½ tsp
Red chilli powder	½ tsp
Coriander powder	1½ tsp
Garam masala powder	½ tsp
Dry mango powder (*amchur*)	¾ tsp
Oil	2 tbsp

METHOD

1. In a pressure cooker heat oil and add cumin seeds. When it become brown, add tomatoes, ginger and green chillies.
2. Fry till the tomatoes are soft and the oil separates.
3. Add all the spices except *amchur* and garam masala powder. Fry for 4-5 minutes.
4. Add potatoes and enough water to make a gravy (use two cups of water).
5. Close the lid and cook for 10-15 minutes till potatoes are cooked.
6. Pour into a serving dish and mix *amchur* and *garam masala* powders.
7. Garnish with coriander leaves and serve hot.

PALAK METHI CHAMAN

(Dry spinach and fenugreek)

INGREDIENTS

Spinach/*palak,* chopped	2 cups
Fresh fenugreek leaves (*methi*), chopped	1 cup
Onion, chopped	1
Tomatoes	2
Ginger, chopped	1 tbsp
Red chilli powder	½ tsp
Coriander powder	1 tsp
Dry mango powder (*amchur*)	1 tsp
Cumin seeds	½ tsp
Oil	1½ tsp
Salt	to taste
Sugar	½ tsp

METHOD

1. Heat oil in a pan, add cumin seeds and chopped onions. Fry till the onions are golden brown and add sugar.
2. Add one chopped tomato to this and fry till soft.
3. Add all the spices except *amchur* powder. Fry for sometime.
4. Add spinach and *methi*. Cover and cook till they are done.
5. Cut and chop the other tomato into big pieces and add.
6. Add *amchur* powder. Fry for 5 minutes and serve hot.

Note: You could add 1-2 tsp of fresh cream for a richer taste.

DRY MOONG DAL

(Savoury green gram)

INGREDIENTS

Washed green gram, split (*moong dal*)	1 cup
Salt	to taste
Oil	½ tsp
Cumin seeds	½ tsp
Green chillies, chopped	1-2
Turmeric powder	½ tsp
Asofoetida (*hing*)	a pinch
Coriander powder	1½ tsp
Red chilli powder	½ tsp
Lime juice	2 tbsp

METHOD

1. Soak the *dal* in water for half-an-hour.
2. Heat oil in a pan and fry asafoetida and cumin seeds till the seeds turn brown.
3. Now add *dal* and all the spices.
4. Add a little water and cover and cook.
5. Stir two or three times.
6. When *dal* is soft, add lime juice and serve hot.

VEGETABLE BIRYANI

INGREDIENTS

Rice	1 cup
Onion	1 chopped
Carrot, diced	1
Beans, chopped finely	1 cup
Cauliflower (cut into small pieces)	1 small
Peas (shelled)	½ cup
Bay leaves	1-2
Cinnamon	1-2 sticks
Cloves	2-3
Cardamoms	2
Cumin seeds	½ tsp
Salt	to taste
Garam masala	1 tsp
Green chillies, cut into julienne	1-2
Oil/*ghee*	2 tsp
Saffron (*kesar*), mixed in water	a few strands

METHOD

1. Wash the rice and soak for 10-15 minutes.
2. In a heated vessel, add some oil or *ghee* and put cumin seeds.
3. When the seeds turn brown, add cinnamon, bay leaves, cloves and onion.
4. Fry the onion till it becomes golden brown. Then add all the vegetables and fry for sometime.
5. Add rice, salt, cardamoms, *garam masala* powder and green chillies.
6. Mix nicely by adding 2 cups of water and *kesar*.
7. Cover tightly. After 15-20 minutes, when it is done, serve hot with plain *raita*.

Mughlai Menu
Gobi Mussallam, Shahi Paneer, Handi Biryani and Bundi Ladoo

Kashmiri Menu
Barith Marchavangun, Nadur Roganjosh and Naan

Contemporary Menu 4
Raw Mango Panna, Masala Bhindi, Suji Halwa and Alu Gravy

PLAIN RAITA

INGREDIENTS

Curd	2 cups
Salt, black pepper,	to taste
Red chilli and chaat masala powders	to taste

METHOD

1. Strain the curd for half-an-hour.
2. Mix all the ingredients, chill and serve.

KHASTA ROTI

INGREDIENTS

Wheatflour (*atta*)	1½ cup
Semolina	1 cup
Salt	to taste
Carom seeds	1 tsp
Oil	2 tsp
Clarified butter/*ghee*	2 tbsp

METHOD

1. Make a dough by mixing all the ingredients (except *ghee*) and water.
2. Roll out *rotis* with a rolling pin and bake them in the *tandoor* or oven/grill golden brown.
3. Smear with *ghee* and serve hot.

RICE KHEER

(Rice pudding)

INGREDIENTS

Milk	5½ cups
Fine basmati rice	½ cup
Sugar	¾ cup
Cardamom (syrup or crushed)	½ tsp
Saffron (*kesar*)	4-5 strands
Almonds, peeled, chopped and soaked in water	2 tbsp

METHOD

1. Soak the rice for ½ an hour.
2. Boil the milk and add rice. Keep stirring on slow fire for 1-1½ hours till milk becomes thick.
3. Add cardamom, saffron and sugar. Keep stirring for another 10 minutes.
4. Garnish with almonds and serve hot.
5. For cold *kheer*, cool at room temperature and keep in the freezer to chill and serve.

MENU

9

Mushroom Soup
Fruit Salad
Lauki Kofta Curry
Dry Tori
Peas Puri
Tri-Coloured Rice
Papad Raita
Sugar Parantha with Vanilla Ice Cream

MUSHROOM SOUP

INGREDIENTS

Button mushrooms	2 cups
Onion, chopped	1
Butter	2 tsp
Salt and pepper	to taste
Lime juice	1 tsp
Parsley, chopped	1 tsp
Dill leaves	a few

METHOD

1. Wash and chop the mushrooms. Heat the butter, fry the mushrooms and onion for 1 minute. Keep some mushrooms aside.

2. Add 4 cups of water to the fried mushrooms and onion slices; cook for sometime. When cooked, blend in a liquidiser and strain.

3. Add dill leaves and 2 tbsp of chopped mushrooms, salt, pepper, and lime juice to the strained liquid/puree. Boil and cook for 2-3 minutes.

4. Garnish with parsley and serve hot.

FRUIT SALAD

INGREDIENTS

Oranges	2
Banana	1
Cherries	a few
Pineapple slices	2
Salad leaves	a few
Lemon juice	few drops

FOR DRESSING:

Orange juice	2 tbsp
Pineapple juice	2 tbsp
Lemon juice	4 tsp
Water	2 tsp
Egg	½
Cream	5 tbsp

METHOD

TO MAKE DRESSING:

1. Heat fruit juices and water.

2. Beat egg slightly and pour into a double boiler.

3. Add sugar to egg and then the hot fruit juice and cook till it thickens (thickness should be custard-like).

4. Cool. Add whipped cream. It is now ready to serve.

FOR SALAD:

Add all chopped fruits to this dressing and serve chilled.

LAUKI KOFTA CURRY

(Bottle gourd cutlet curry)

FOR CUTLETS (*KOFTA*):

INGREDIENTS

Bottle gourd, (*lauki*)	150 gm/2 cups grated
Gramflour	½ cup
Salt, red chilli powder	to taste
Garam masala powder	to taste
Dry mango powders (*amchur*)	to taste
Breadcrumbs	4 tbsp

METHOD

1. Peel and wash the *lauki*. Grate and squeeze out extra water.
2. Mix in all the spices, gramflour and breadcrumbs.
3. Make walnut-sized balls. Deep-fry till golden brown.

FOR CURRY:

INGREDIENTS

Onions, grated	2
Tomatoes, grated	3
Ginger paste	1 tbsp
Salt	to taste
Red chilli powder	½ tsp
Dry mango powder (*amchur*)	½ tsp
Garam masala powder	½ tsp
Coriander powder	1½ tsp
Coriander leaves, chopped	a few
Green chillies, chopped	2
Oil	2 tbsp
Turmeric powder	½ tsp

METHOD

1. Heat oil in a pan; add onions and fry till golden brown.
2. Add tomatoes, ginger and green chillies. Fry till the oil separates.
3. Add all the spices and fry for 5 minutes.
4. Pour the curry into a serving dish.
5. Garnish with coriander leaves.
6. Soak the cutlets in the curry.
7. Serve hot.

DRY TORI

(Dry ridge gourd)

INGREDIENTS

Ridge gourd (*tori*), cut	2 cups
Tomato, chopped	1
Salt	to taste
Red chilli powder	1 tsp
Coriander powder	1 tsp
Turmeric powder	½ tsp
Oil	2 tbsp
Cumin seeds	½ tsp

METHOD

1. Peel, wash and cut the *tori* in big pieces.
2. Heat oil in a wok, add cumin seeds and after one minute add the *tori* pieces along with salt, red chilli, coriander and turmeric powders. Stir well, cover and cook on slow fire for 10 minutes or till the *toris* are half cooked.
3. Add chopped tomatoes and cook for another 5 minutes. Serve hot.

PEA PURI

INGREDIENTS

FOR *PURI*:

Wheatflour (*atta*)	2 cups
Refined flour	4 tbsp
Salt	to taste
Melted fat	1 tsp

FOR FILLING:

Peas	3 tbsp
Green chilli	½
Coriander leaves	few
Cumin seeds	1/8 tsp
Red chilli *garam masala* powders	a pinch each
Oil	for frying

METHOD

1. Boil the peas. Chop the green chilli and coriander leaves. Mix together, the spices for filling along with chopped chilli and coriander well.

2. Sift the refined flour and wheatflour and add salt and rub in the melted fat.

3. Make a soft dough using water. Leave aside for half an-hour.

4. Knead the dough again using a little fat.

5. Divide into 9-10 portions and shape into balls.

6. Make a depression in the centre of each ball and fill in the peas mixture and then again shape into a ball.

7. Roll into flat round discs using oil.

8. Deep-fry discs in hot oil on both sides and serve hot, as an accompaniment.

TRI-COLOURED RICE

INGREDIENTS

Rice, boiled	3 cups
Spinach puree	½ cup
Tomato puree	½ cup
Turmeric powder	1 tsp
Salt	to taste
Black pepper	1 tsp
Red chilli powder	1 tsp
Garam masala powder	1 tsp
Sugar	½ tsp
Coriander leaves, chopped	a few
Green chillies, chopped	1 tbsp

METHOD

1. Divide the cooked rice into three equal portions.

2. To one portion add tomato puree, salt, red chilli powder and sugar and mix well.

3. To the second portion, add spinach puree, salt and black pepper and mix well. Keep aside.

4. To the third portion, add turmeric powder, salt and *garam masala* powder and mix well.

5. On a serving dish put the rice in three layers and serve.

PAPAD RAITA

INGREDIENTS

Curd	3 cups
Salt	to taste
Red chilli powder	½ tsp
Roasted cumin seed powder	½ tsp
Papads	2

METHOD

1. Beat the curd and mix all the spices.
2. Roast *papads* on slow fire or in a microwave or a toaster. Crush into small pieces.
3. Before serving mix crushed *papad* with beaten curd. Garnish with chopped coriander leaves and serve.

SUGAR PARANTHA WITH VANILLA ICE CREAM

INGREDIENTS

Wheatflour (*atta*)	2 cups
Sugar	6 tbsp
Clarified butter/*ghee*	for frying
Vanilla ice cream	4 scoops

METHOD

1. Make a dough with wheatflour and water. Keep aside for 10-15 minutes.
2. Divide the dough in 5-6 portions, roll out one portion and apply *ghee*. Fill with 3 tsp of sugar and close. Roll again using dry flour. Repeat for the rest of the dough.
3. Fry them from both sides on a hot griddle with *ghee* till sides turn golden brown and crispy.
4. Cut the *paranthas* in triangular shapes and serve with vanilla ice cream.

10

MENU

Cauliflower Soup
Laccha Salad
Rajmah Curry
Corn and Spinach
Dry Paneer
Plain Fried Rice
Roomali Roti
Boondi Raita
Ice Cream Apple Paradise

CAULIFLOWER SOUP

INGREDIENTS

Cauliflower	1 small floret
Onion, chopped	1 small
Milk	2 cups
Salt and pepper	to taste
Tomato, cut into pieces	1
Carrot, chopped and boiled	1
Butter/oil	1 tsp

METHOD

1. Boil the cauliflower, milk and tomato slices in 3 cups of water.
2. When cooked, blend in a liquidiser and strain.
3. Heat the butter and fry the onion for ½ a minute. Add the cauliflower liquid and carrots; boil and cook for 5 minutes.
4. Add salt and pepper and serve hot.

LACCHA SALAD

INGREDIENTS

Red cabbage, grated	½
Carrot, grated	½
Cucumber, grated	1
Radish, grated	1
Salad leaves	few
Sprouts	2 tbsp
Pomegranate seeds	2 tbsp
Cornflakes	1 tbsp

FOR DRESSING:

Lemon juice	2 tbsp
Salt	to taste
Honey	few drops
Chopped coriander leaves	1 tsp
Red chilli powder	½ tsp

METHOD

Mix everything. Garnish with cornflakes and serve.

RAJMAH CURRY

(Red kidney beans curry)

INGREDIENTS

Red kidney beans (*rajmah*)	½ cup
Onion, grated	2
Tomato, grated	2
Garlic	2 cloves
Ginger	1 tbsp
Green chillies, chopped	2
Salt	to taste
Coriander powder	2 tsp
Turmeric powder	½ tsp
Garam masala powder	½ tsp
Red chilli powder	½ tsp
Dry mango powder (*amchur*)	1 tsp
Coriander leaves, chopped	a few
Oil	2 tbsp
Sugar	a pinch
Cumin seeds	½ tsp
Bay leaves	2

METHOD

1. Wash the *rajmah* and soak for 10 hours or overnight.
2. Pressure-cook with salt and turmeric powder and 2 cups of water.
3. Heat oil in a pan, add cumin seeds and bay leaves. After 1 minute add onions, ginger and garlic. Fry till onions turn golden brown.
4. Add tomatoes and cook till the oil separates. Add all the spices and a pinch of sugar. Fry for 4-5 minutes.
5. Add cooked *rajmah*, stir and cook for 10-15 minutes on slow fire.
6. Garnish with coriander leaves and serve hot.

CORN AND SPINACH

INGREDIENTS

Spinach, chopped	2 cups
Fresh boiled corn cobs	½ cup
Onion, grated	1, big
Ginger paste	1 tsp
Garlic paste	1 tsp
Tomato, pureed	1, big
Salt	to taste
Red chilli powder	¼ tsp
Dry mango powder (*amchur*)	½ tsp
Garam masala powder	½ tsp
Coriander powder	1 tsp
Oil	2 tsp
Fresh cream	for garnish

METHOD

1. Heat oil in a pan, add grated onion, ginger and garlic pastes and fry till onion becomes light brown in colour.
2. Add tomato puree and fry for 4-5 minutes.
3. Boil the spinach and grind to a paste. Keep aside.
4. Add all the spices to onion and tomato puree.
5. Fry for sometime. Add spinach puree and corn.
6. Keep on fire for 10 minutes; if required add a little water.
7. Garnish with fresh cream or white butter and serve hot.

DRY PANEER

(Cottage cheese with capsicum)

INGREDIENTS

Cottage cheese/*paneer,* cut into big cubes	10-15 cubes
Capsicum, cut into cubes	1, big
Onions, thinly sliced	2
Tomatoes, thinly sliced	2
Red chilli paste	1 tbsp
Dry mango powder (*amchur*)	1 tsp
Garam masala powder	½ tsp
Oil	2 tsp
Salt	to taste

METHOD

1. Heat oil in a pan, fry the onions till golden brown.
2. Add tomatoes and fry till soft.
3. Add all the spices except *amchur* and fry for 2 minutes.
4. Add cottage cheese cubes and capsicum, cover and leave on slow fire for ten minutes.
5. Add *amchur* and serve hot.

PLAIN FRIED RICE

INGREDIENTS

Rice	1 cup
Oil	2 tbsp
Cumin seeds	1 tsp
Salt	to taste
Garam masala powder	1 tsp
Bay leaves	2
Cloves	2
Cinnamon sticks	2
Onions, sliced and fried to golden brown	2

METHOD

1. Wash the rice and soak for 10-15 minutes.
2. Heat oil in a thick-bottomed vessel. Add cumin seeds, bay leaves, cloves, cinnamon sticks and fry for 2 minutes.
3. Add rice and 2 cups of water. Add salt and *garam masala* powder. Cover and leave on slow fire till the rice is cooked.
4. Garnish with fried onions and serve hot.

ROOMALI ROTI

INGREDIENTS

Refined flour	2 cups
Curd	½ cup
Milk	1 cup
Butter	4 tsp
Castor sugar	2 tsp
Yeast, soaked in water	2 tsp
Salt	to taste
Clarified butter/*ghee*	2-4 tsp
Egg	1

METHOD

1. Sieve the flour and add sugar. Beat the egg and add it to the flour.
2. Rub in butter.
3. Add yeast. Add curd and make a soft dough using milk. Add water if required.
4. Knead well for 5 minutes.
5. Add 2 tsp of melted *ghee* and knead again.
6. Keep the dough covered for 3-4 hrs.
7. Divide the dough into 5-10 balls and shape into rounds with fingers.
8. Roll them out into very big-sized but very thin *rotis*.

9. Heat a *tandoor* or grill for 30-45 minutes. Put one big-sized *roti* on the *tandoor*. Cook till both sides are light brown. Repeat for the rest.

10. Fold and serve hot.

BOONDI RAITA

INGREDIENTS

Gramflour	1½ tbsp
Curd	2 cups
Oil	for frying
Salt, red chilli powder,	to taste
Roasted and powdered	to taste
cumin seeds	to taste
Sugar	½ tsp
Black salt	½ tsp

METHOD

1. Add salt and red chilli powder and sufficient water to gramflour to make a batter of dropping consistency.

2. Beat the batter with a spoon till light and fluffy.

3. Heat oil in a wok till it starts to smoke and pour the batter through a perforated ladle into the oil.

4. You will get small round balls or *boondis*. Fry the *boondis* till golden brown. Remove from fire and soak in water for 15-20 minutes.

5. Beat the curd. Add *boondi,* salt, red chilli powder, sugar and black salt and serve.

Note: Boondi *is also available in the market.*

ICE CREAM APPLE PARADISE

INGREDIENTS

Cooking apples	4 nos
Lemon Juice	1 tbsp
Castor Sugar	4 tbsp
Vanilla Ice Cream	4 scoops
Fresh cream	250 gms
Black Currant Jam	2 tbsp
Water	¼ cup

METHOD

1. Peel the apples and cut into small pieces.

2. Boil water, lemon juice and sugar.

3. Allow to cool.

4. Place ice-cream at the centre of each serving dish, then surround with the soft apple mixture. Decorate with black currant jam and whipped cream. Serve immediately.

11

MENU

Clear Vegetable Broth
Peas and Mushroom Salad
Dahi Ka Alu
Green Baby Corn
Banana Kuchumber
Cucumber Raita
Cottage Cheese Pilaff
Ajwain Roti
Watermelon Sorbet
Til Ladoo

CLEAR VEGETABLE BROTH

INGREDIENTS

Celery	2 thick pieces, finely chopped
Carrot	1 large, chopped
Onion	1, cut into rings
Chopped parsley	2 tbsp
Bay leaf	1
Water	5 cups
Butter	2 tsp
Salt & Pepper	to taste

METHOD

1. Heat the butter, add the bay leaf and onion. Cook for 1 minute.
2. Add the vegetables and cook for 3-4 minutes.
3. Add the water and boil for 15-20 minutes.
4. Add the chopped parsley, salt and pepper. Serve hot.

PEAS AND MUSHROOM SALAD

INGREDIENTS

Peas, boiled	1 cup
Mushrooms, boiled	2 cups
Green chilli, chopped	1 tbsp
Spring onion with leaves, chopped	1 cup
Ginger, grated	1 tbsp
Salt	to taste
Black pepper	2 tsp
Oil or butter	2 tbsp
Lime juice	1 tbsp

METHOD

1. Heat oil in a pan, add ginger and spring onion and fry for sometime.
2. Add peas, mushrooms, green chillies, salt and black pepper and sauté. Mix well.
3. Add lime juice and serve.

DAHI KA ALU

INGREDIENTS

Potatoes, boiled, peeled and cut into small pieces	2
Curd	2 cups
Gramflour	1 tsp
Salt	to taste
Turmeric powder	½ tsp
Asafoetida (*hing*)	a pinch
Cumin seeds	½ tsp
Red chilli powder	½ tsp
Oil	2 tbsp

METHOD

1. Beat curd by adding gramflour.
2. Heat oil in a pan and fry asafoetida and cumin seeds. When the cumin seeds turn

brown, add chilli powder. After half-a-minute add beaten curd and a little water.

3. Keep stirring till it boils.

4. Add potatoes, boil and cook for 10 minutes on slow fire. Serve hot.

GREEN BABY CORN

INGREDIENTS

Baby corn, cut into small pieces	10
Spinach, chopped	4 cups
Onion, ground into paste	1
Ginger paste	1 tbsp
Garlic paste	1 tbsp
Tomatoes, boiled and pureed	2
Salt	to taste
Red chilli powder	½ tsp
Garam masala powder	½ tsp
Coriander powder	1 tsp
Dry mango powder (*amchur*)	1 tsp
Cream (optional)	2 tbsp
Oil	2 tbsp

METHOD

1. Boil the chopped spinach and make a puree after grinding.

2. Boil the chopped baby corn.

3. In a heated pan, put some oil and add onion, ginger and garlic. Fry till onions are golden brown.

4. Add tomatoes and fry for 10 minutes till oil separates. Add all the spices and fry for sometime.

5. Add spinach puree and baby corn. Cover and cook for 10 minutes.

6. Garnish with cream and serve hot.

BANANA KUCHUMBER

(*Banana salad*)

INGREDIENTS

Bananas, chopped	2
Onion, chopped	1
Tomato	1
Salt	to taste
Lime juice	2 tbsp
Chaat masala	1 tbsp
Green chilli, chopped (optional)	1
Coriander leaves, chopped	a few

METHOD

Mix all the ingredients, chill and serve.

CUCUMBER RAITA

INGREDIENTS

Curd	2 cups
Cucumber, grated	5 tbsp
Salt, red chilli powder	to taste
Roasted and powdered	to taste
cumin seeds	to taste

METHOD

1. Beat the curd and add grated cucumber.

2. Sprinkle salt, red chilli and cumin seed powder and serve.

COTTAGE CHEESE PILAFF

INGREDIENTS

Rice	1 cup
Cottage cheese/*paneer,* cut into cubes	5 tbsp
Onion, chopped	5 tbsp
Clarified butter/*ghee*	1 tbsp and for frying
Water	2 cups
Salt, cumin seeds, cloves and	to taste
bay leaves	to taste

METHOD

1. Clean, wash the rice and soak in water.
2. Heat *ghee,* fry cottage cheese cubes till golden brown. Remove and fry onion slices to golden brown.
3. Add the whole spices and fry for a few minutes.
4. Add the rice and fry for 3-4 minutes. Add water.
5. Bring to a boil, add fried cheese cubes and cook till done.
6. Serve hot with curry.

AJWAIN ROTI

(Carom-flavoured roti)

INGREDIENTS

Wheatflour (*atta*)	2 cups
Salt	to taste
Carom seeds	1 tsp
Red chilli powder	¾ tsp
Dry mango powder (*amchur*)	½ tsp
Oil	1 tbsp
Clarified or white butter	to taste

METHOD

1. Make a dough by adding enough water to the flour and some salt.
2. Keep aside for 10-15 minutes.
3. With a rolling pin, roll out one small portion, apply oil. Sprinkle salt, red chilli powder, carom and *amchur.*
4. Close and roll it again with the help of dry flour. Repeat for the rest of the dough.
5. Roast the *rotis* on a hot griddle till golden brown from both sides.
6. Apply butter and serve hot.

WATERMELON SORBET

INGREDIENTS

Watermelon	1, small (weighting 1½-2 kg)
Sifted icing sugar	1½ cups
Juice	of 1 lemon
Mint	few sprigs

METHOD

1. Discard the seeds and scoop out the flesh from the watermelon. Preserve the shell and cut into 4 wedges.
2. Place the shell wedges in a freezer-proof bowl of the same size and shape. Chill in the freezer.
3. Place the flesh in a blender with the sugar and lemon juice and blend until smooth.
4. Pour into a rigid container and freeze for 3-4 hours. Invert into a chilled bowl and whisk until fluffy.
5. Invert the melon shells on this and smoothen the top. Cover with silver foil and freeze until solid.
6. Decorate with mint sprigs and serve chilled.

TIL LADOO

(Sesame-flavoured sweets)

INGREDIENTS

Sesame seeds (*til*)	1 cup
Sugar	1 cup
Wholemilk fudge (*khoya*), grated	5 tbsp

METHOD

1. Clean *til* seeds and pound to a paste with a pestle and mortar.
2. Add sifted sugar and grated fudge.
3. Pound the mixture again, till mixed well.
4. With your hands, form into medium-sized balls or *ladoos*.

MENU

12

Carrot Soup
Orange Yogurt Salad
Spilt Urad Dal
Spinach Mushroom
Methi Alu
Gramflour and Spinach Parantha
Fruit Raita
Tomato Rice
Peanut Chikki

CARROT SOUP

INGREDIENTS

Carrots	4 cups
Tomatoes	2, big
Green gram (*moong dal*)	1 tbsp
Skimmed milk	1 cup
Salt and pepper	to taste
Dill leaves, chopped	a few

METHOD

1. Cut the carrots and tomatoes into big pieces.
2. Add 3 cups of water, *moong dal* and salt and cook in a pressure cooker.
3. When cooked, blend in a liquidiser and strain.
4. Heat milk and add to the soup, mix well.
5. Add pepper and dill leaves. Boil and serve hot.

ORANGE YOGURT SALAD

INGREDIENTS

Cucumber, chopped	1
Carrot, chopped	1
Apple, chopped	1
Lettuce leaves, cut into halves	6-8
Thick yogurt	1 cup
Tang orange powder (available in the market)	4 tbsp
Mint leaves, finely chopped	4 tbsp
Salt	to taste

METHOD

1. Beat yogurt till creamy and smooth. Add *Tang* orange powder, mint leaves and salt and mix well.
2. Add cucumber, carrots and apple to the yogurt dressing.
3. Spread lettuce leaves on a flat dish and pour salad mixture neatly on top.

Spilt Urad Dal

(Dry black gram)

INGREDIENTS

Split black gram (*urad dal*)	1 cup
Salt	to taste
Ginger, chopped	1 tbsp
Green chillies, chopped	2
Red chilli powder	½ tsp
Cumin seeds	½ tsp
Asafoetida (*hing*)	a pinch
Oil	2 tbsp
Lime juice	1 tbsp

METHOD

1. Wash the *dal* and soak for 15-20 minutes.
2. Pressure-cook *dal* with salt till soft. Add lime juice and keep aside.
3. Heat oil in a pan and add asafoetida and cumin seeds. After 1 minute, add ginger and green chillies. Again, after a minute add red chilli powder.
4. Pour this on the *dal* and serve hot.

Spinach Mushroom

INGREDIENTS

Spinach, chopped	2 cups
Mushrooms, cut into small pieces	1 cup
Onions, made into paste	2
Ginger paste	1 tbsp
Garlic paste	1 tbsp
Tomato puree	1 cup
Salt	to taste
Red chilli powder	½ tsp
Dry mango powder (*amchur*)	½ tsp
Garam masala powder	½ tsp
Coriander powder	1 tsp
Oil	2 tbsp
Fresh cream	1 tbsp

METHOD

1. Boil the spinach, blend into a puree and keep aside.
2. Boil the mushrooms in salted water and keep aside.
3. Heat oil in a pan, add onion paste and fry till golden brown.
4. Add ginger, garlic pastes and tomato puree; fry till oil separates.
5. Add all the spices and fry for 2-3 minutes. Add spinach puree and mushrooms.
6. Cover and leave on slow flame for 5 minutes.
7. Garnish with fresh cream and serve hot.

Methi Alu

(Fenugreek-flavoured potatoes)

INGREDIENTS

Potatoes, peeled and cut into cubes	2, big
Fresh fenugreek leaves, washed and chopped	2 cups
Salt	to taste
Red chilli powder	½ tsp
Coriander powder	1½ tsp
Garam masala powder	½ tsp
Turmeric powder	½ tsp
Dry mango powder (*amchur*)	1 tsp
Oil	2 tbsp
Cumin seeds	½ tsp
Asafoetida (*hing*)	a pinch

METHOD

1. Heat oil in a pan, fry asafoetida and cumin seeds. After a minute, add cubed potatoes and fenugreek leaves.
2. Add all the spices except *garam masala* and *amchur* powders.
3. Mix well; cover and leave on slow flame till potatoes are soft.
4. Add *amchur* and *garam masala* powder, mix well and serve hot.

Gramflour and Spinach Parantha

INGREDIENTS

Wheatflour (*atta*)	1 cup
Gramflour	½ cup
Onions	2
Spinach, washed and chopped	1 cup
Green chillies	2
Oil	for frying
Salt, red chilli powder	to taste
Amchur and *garam masala* powders	to taste

METHOD

1. Mix wheatflour, gramflour, chopped onions, green chillies, spinach, salt, chilli powder, *garam masala* and *amchur* powders.
2. Using water, make a soft dough and leave aside for a while.
3. Knead the dough and divide into 4 balls.
4. Roll one ball into a small round. Apply a little oil, fold again and roll out again into a round shape.
5. Fry from both sides on a hot griddle. Repeat for the other dough balls.
6. Serve hot with curd.

FRUIT RAITA

INGREDIENTS

Curd	3 cups
Sugar	2 tsp
Mixed fruits, sliced (bananas, pineapple, strawberry, apples mangoes, cherries, oranges, if available)	1 cup

METHOD

1. Beat the curd. Add sugar and cut fruits.
2. Mix well. Serve chilled

Note: You could garnish with dry fruits if you wish.

TOMATO RICE

INGREDIENTS

Rice, boiled	2 cups
Onions, chopped	2
Tomatoes, chopped	2
Cumin seeds	½ tsp
Salt	to taste
Dry mango powder (*amchur*)	½ tsp
Garam masala powder	½ tsp
Oil	2 tbsp

METHOD

1. Heat oil in a pan and fry cumin seeds.
2. When they turn brown, add onion and fry till soft.
3. Add tomatoes. Fry till soft.
4. Add rice, salt, *amchur* and *garam masala* powders.
5. Fry for 5 minutes and serve hot.

PEANUT CHIKKI

(Sweet peanut biscuit)

INGREDIENTS

Roasted peanuts	2½ cups
Jaggery/sugar	2 cups
Butter	2½ tbsp

METHOD

1. Heat sugar/jaggery with ½ cup of water until thick. Boil the syrup until it becomes of a hard consistency. (Test its consistency by putting a drop in cold water; it should crack after you take it out.)
2. Add peanuts and mix thoroughly.
3. Grease a tray and spread the mixture, evenly to 1cm thickness.
4. Cut into squares when cooled and store in an airtight container.

13

MENU

Cream of Mixed Vegetable Soup
Baby Vegetable Salad
Sindhi Curry
Tawa Baingan
Chana Lauki and Dal
Spinach Puri
Potato Halwa

CREAM OF MIXED VEGETABLE SOUP

INGREDIENTS

Tomatoes	2
Carrots	2
Onion	2
Beans	5-6
Green peas, shelled	½ cup
Butter	1 tsp
Milk	¾ cup
Cauliflower, chopped	½ tsp
Cornflour	1 tsp
Grated Cheese	2 tsp
Salt and pepper	to taste

METHOD

1. Wash, peel and cut vegetables into small pieces. Add 4 cups of water and cook till vegetables are tender.

2. Pass the mixture through a sieve.

3. Make white sauce using butter, cornflour and milk (as given in the Basic Recipes section).

4. Add strained mixture to white sauce and mix well.

5. Season with salt and pepper and serve hot with grated cheese on top.

BABY VEGETABLE SALAD

INGREDIENTS

Baby potatoes	10
Baby carrots	12-14
Baby cucumber or zucchini	12-14
Baby cabbage	10
Baby onion	15
Baby corn	13-15
Baby tomatoes	10
Oil	2 tbsp
Chilli sauce	2 tbsp
Garlic pulp	1 tbsp
Ginger pulp	1 tbsp
Salt	1 tbsp
Crushed dry red chillies	1 tbsp
Roasted sesame seeds	2 tbsp

METHOD

1. Steam or boil all the baby vegetables except onions and tomatoes. Do not overboil. The vegetables should be just tender.

2. Heat oil in a deep round-bottomed frying pan. Add the baby onions, fry until the onions turn golden brown. Lower the heat and add chilli sauce, garlic, ginger and salt. Take care not to burn the mixture.

3. Add the cooked vegetables and baby tomatoes. Stir, while cooking for about 2 minutes.

4. Add the crushed red chillies. Garnish with roasted sesame seeds and serve.

SINDHI CURRY

INGREDIENTS

Gramflour	3 tbsp
Mustard seeds	½ tsp
Fenugreek seeds	½ tsp
Cumin seeds	½ tsp
Curry leaves	few
Oil	3 tbsp
Carrot, chopped	1
Lotus stem (*kamal kakari*)	1
Cauliflower	½
Peas, shelled	½ cup
Brinjal	2 small
Lady's finger	4-5
Beans	4-5
Tomatoes	2
Potato	1
Salt	to taste
Whole red chillies	2-3
Red chilli powder	1 tsp
Garam masala powder	1 tsp
Tamarind water	½ cup
Jaggery, powdered	2 tbsp

METHOD

1. Heat oil in a wok. Add cumin, mustard and fenugreek seeds. When they all start to crackle or brown, add curry leaves and whole red chillies.
2. Add gramflour and fry till it is brown. Add 5 cups of water; stir continuously till it boils. Add salt and leave on slow flame for half an-hour.
3. Cut all the vegetables (except lotus stem, potato and cauliflower) in small pieces and add to the curry. Deep-fry lotus stem, potato and cauliflower, separately and add to the curry.
4. When the curry becomes thick and all the vegetables turn soft, add tamarind water and *garam masala* powder. Add jaggery and cook for 5 minutes.
5. Heat a little oil separately. Fry red chilli powder for a minute. Pour it on the curry.
6. Serve hot with plain rice and *boondi*.

TAWA BAINGAN

(Spicy brinjal roasted on a griddle)

INGREDIENTS

Brinjal	1 big
Salt	to taste
Red chilli powder	1 tsp
Dry mango powder (*amchur*)	1 tsp
Garam masala powder	1 tsp
Lime juice	1 tbsp
Coriander leaves, chopped	a few
Green chillies, chopped	2
Oil	for shallow-frying

METHOD

1. Wash and slice the brinjal in pieces about ½ inch in thickness.
2. Slit the pieces from the centre.
3. On a heated griddle (*tawa*), fry the brinjal pieces in oil from both sides till golden brown.
4. Sprinkle all the spices and lime juice.
5. Garnish with coriander leaves and green chillies and serve hot.

CHANA LAUKI AND DAL

(Bottle gourd and Bengal gram dal)

INGREDIENTS

Bengal gram (*chana dal*)	1 cup
Bottle gourd (*lauki*), peeled and cut into cubes	1 cup
Salt	to taste
Turmeric powder	½ tsp
Bay leaves	2

FOR SEASONING OR *TADKA*

Oil	2 tbsp
Coriander powder	2 tsp
Green chillies, chopped	2
Dry mango powder (*amchur*)	1 tsp
Red chilli powder	½ tsp

METHOD

1. Wash the *dal* and soak in water for 15 minutes.
2. Pressure-cook the *dal* with bay leaves, *lauki,* salt, turmeric powder and 3 cups of water.
3. Heat oil and add green chillies, coriander and red chilli powders. Fry for one minute and pour this on the *dal.*
4. Mix *amchur* powder in cooked *dal* and serve hot.

SPINACH PURI

INGREDIENTS

Wheatflour (*atta*)	1 cup
Melted fat	1 tsp
Spinach, chopped	1 cup
Dry mango powder (*amchur*) salt,	to taste
Red chilli powder	to taste
Garam masala powder	to taste
Oil	for frying

METHOD

1. Wash the spinach leaves and cook them in a covered pan for 5 minutes on low heat.
2. Uncover the pan and dry out any liquid which is left.
3. Grind the cooked spinach to a fine paste.
4. Sift the wheatflour.
5. Add the spices to the flour and rub the melted fat.
6. Mix the spinach paste in the flour and make a dough (if needed, add water).
7. Leave the dough covered for 15 minutes or half-an-hour.
8. Knead the dough again for a few minutes. Divide the dough into 5-6 parts and shape into balls.
9. Roll each ball into a thin circle (*puri*) using oil.
10. Heat oil in a wok and fry each *puri* on both sides.
11. Serve with *raita*, chutney, pickle etc.

Potato Halwa

(Potato pudding)

INGREDIENTS

Potatoes	**1 kg**
Sugar	**¾ cup**
Saffron (*kesar*)	**a few strands**
Clarified butter/*ghee*	**1 cup**

METHOD

1. Boil, peel and mash the potatoes.

2. Heat *ghee* in a wok. Add potatoes and fry till they change colour (approx.: 45 minutes).

3. Add sugar and saffron. Fry for some more time. Serve hot.

14

Moong Dal Aur Palak Shorba
Paneer, Apple Pineapple Salad
Stuffed Capsicum
Alu Matar Dry
Spicy Vegetable Rice
Mooli Parantha
Coconut Burfi

MOONG DAL AUR PALAK SHORBA

(Green gram and spinach soup)

INGREDIENTS

Green gram (*moong dal*)	½ cup
Spinach, chopped	½ cup
Salt	to taste
Turmeric powder	½ tsp
Lime juice	1 tsp

METHOD

1. Wash the *dal* and boil with 3 cups of water, salt and turmeric powder.
2. Blend in the mixer and strain.
3. Add spinach and cook for 10 minutes.
4. Add lime juice and serve hot.

PANEER, APPLE AND PINEAPPLE SALAD

INGREDIENTS

Cottage cheese/*paneer*	60 gm/15 pieces when chopped
Apple	½
Pineapple slices	2
Cucumber	½
Grapes	a bunch
Grapes	¼ tbsp
Walnuts	½ tbsp
Fresh curd	½ cup/50 gm
Sugar	1 tsp
Sugar, salt and grated carrot	for garnishing
Tomato ketchup (optional)	½ tsp
Salad leaves	few

METHOD

1. Slice apple, pineapple, grapes, cucumber and *paneer*.
2. Beat the cream and curd, sugar and ketchup. Mix well and chill in the refrigerator.
3. Drain the fruits thoroughly and add walnuts, salt and sugar. Add this to the chilled cream dressing and mix well.
4. Serve chilled decorated with grated carrot and salad leaves.

STUFFED CAPSICUM

INGREDIENTS

Capsicums	4
Potatoes	4
Onion, chopped	2 tbsp
Ginger, chopped	1 tsp
Red chilli powder salt and garam masala powder	to taste
Dry mango (*amchur*) powder	1 tsp
Clarified butter/*Ghee*	3 tsp

METHOD

1. Boil, peel and mash potatoes.
2. Heat 1 tsp of *ghee* and add chopped onion slices, ginger, all the spices and mashed potatoes.

3. Fry for 2-3 minutes. Keep aside to cool.

4. Wash capsicums and remove the stalks along with thin slices from the tops.

5. Fill with potato stuffing and replace the top slices.

6. Heat 2 tsp of *ghee* and cook the capsicums in it on slow fire in a covered pan till tender.

ALU MATAR DRY

(Spicy potatoes with peas)

INGREDIENTS

Peas	1 cup
Potatoes, peeled and cut into cubes	2-3
Ginger, chopped	1 tbsp
Green chillies, chopped	1 tbsp
Asafoetida (*hing*)	a pinch
Cumin seeds	½ tsp
Salt	to taste
Coriander powder	2 tsp
Turmeric powder	½ tsp
Red chilli powder	½ tsp
Garam masala powder	½ tsp
Dry mango (*amchur*) powder	½ tsp
Oil	2 tbsp
Coriander leaves, chopped	a few

METHOD

1. Heat oil in a wok, add *hing* and cumin seeds. When the cumin seeds turn brown, add peas and potatoes. Put in all the spices except *amchur* and garam masala powders. Add ginger and chillies.

2. Mix well, cover and leave on slow fire till the potatoes and peas are cooked.

3. Add *garam masala* and *amchur* powders and mix well.

4. Garnish with coriander leaves and serve hot.

SPICY VEGETABLE RICE

INGREDIENTS

Rice, boiled	2
Onion puree	1 cup
Tomato puree	1 cup
Mixed vegetables (cauliflower, peas, carrot, beans), chopped	1 cup
Tomato, cut into cubes	1
Green chillies, chopped	2
Salt	to taste
Red chilli powder	½ tsp
Oil	2
Coriander leaves, chopped	a few
Lime juice	1 tsp
Star-anis seeds	2-3

METHOD

1. Parboil the vegetables and keep it aside.

2. Heat oil in a pan, add onion puree and star-anis seeds and fry till golden brown.

3. Add tomato puree and fry till oil separates.

4. Add salt and red chilli powder and green chillies.

5. Add the vegetables, rice and lime juice and coriander leaves. Mix well and serve hot.

Mooli Parantha

(Parantha stuffed with radish)

INGREDIENTS

FOR PARANTHA:

Wheatflour (*atta*)	2 cups
Water	for making dough
Dry flour	for rolling

FOR STUFFING:

Radish	1 cup
Ginger	a small piece
Green chilli	1
Salt, red chilli, dry mango (*amchur*) and garam masala powders	to taste
Clarified butter/*ghee*	for frying

METHOD

1. Make a thick dough as for making *paranthas*.
2. Grate the radish and ginger. Chop the green chilli and mix them well along with the spices.
3. Divide the dough into 4 balls and then divide each ball into 2 smaller balls.
4. To make the *parantha*, roll out 2 small balls into flat discs. Place the filling on one and cover with the other. Make sure you press the edges and again roll out flat tightly. Repeat for the rest of the balls.
5. Heat a griddle and fry the *parantha* by smearing with *ghee* on both sides.
6. Serve hot with curd, *raita* or *chutney*.

Coconut Burfi

(Coconut-flavoured fudge)

INGREDIENTS

Wholemilk fudge/*khoya*	2 cups
Coconut powder	½ cup
Castor sugar	½ cup
Vetivier (*kewra*) essence	2 drops
Artificial colour (optional)	a few drops

METHOD

1. Grate or mash the *khoya* well.
2. Cook it on slow fire. Remove from fire and add sugar. Cook again on slow fire. Add desiccated coconut powder and cook till the powder leaves the sides of the pan.
3. Add *kewra* essence and colour (if any) and mix well.
4. Spread the mixture on a greased plate.
5. Cut into pieces when cold and set in the refrigerator.

CHAAT MENUS

1. Mix all the ingredients for the dough with water and keep aside.
2. Roll out small, round *puris* and deep-fry till golden brown and fluffy.
3. Mix all the ingredients for the dry filling.
4. Mix all the ingredients for *pani*.
5. Serve *puri*, filling and the *pani* separately.

Note: Puris *for making* panipuris *are also available in the market.*

MENU

1

Panipuri
Alu Chaat
Pav Bhaji
Dahi Gunjiya
Shahi Tukda

PANIPURI

(Crisp flour balls filled with spicy potatoes and white chickpeas)

INGREDIENTS

FOR DOUGH:

Wheatflour (*atta*)	2 cups
Oil	2 tbsp
Salt	to taste

FOR DRY FILLING:

Potatoes, boiled, peeled and chopped	2
White chickpeas	½ cup (boiled with a pinch of salt)
Mint chutney	2 tbsp
Tamarind chutney	2 tbsp
Salt, red chilli powder	½ tsp
Dry mango powder (*amchur*)	½ tsp
Chaat masala (available in the market)	½ tsp

FOR LIQUID FILLING (*PANI*):

Chilled water	2 cups
Salt, *chaat masala*, red chilli powder	to taste
Lime juice	3 tbsp
Mint and tamarind chutneys	to taste

ALU CHAAT

(Spicy potatoes)

INGREDIENTS

Potatoes, boiled and peeled	3
Oil	for shallow-frying
Salt	to taste
Chaat masala	1 tsp
Black pepper powder	1 tsp
Green chillies, chopped	2
Ginger, chopped	1 tsp
Lime juice	juice of 1 lime
Coriander leaves, finely chopped	a sprig

METHOD

1. Cut the potatoes into 1" size pieces.
2. Fry them on a griddle or *tava* till golden brown, using oil.
3. Remove from fire, place on a serving dish and add all other ingredients. Mix well.
4. Garnish with chopped coriander leaves and serve.

Pav Bhaji

(Spicy mashed potatoes and peas in tomato gravy served with bread)

INGREDIENTS

Potatoes, boiled, peeled and mashed	5 cups
Peas, boiled and mashed	1 cup
Tomatoes, chopped	5 cups
Onions, chopped	4
Butter	1½ tbsp
Pavs (small square buns)	4-6
Salt	to taste
Red chilli powder	to taste
Pav bhaji masala, dry mango powder (*amchur*)	to taste
Clarified butter (*ghee*)	2 tbsp
Lemon slice	1
Onions, finely chopped	2

METHOD

1. Heat *ghee* in a pan and fry the onions till soft.

2. Add the mashed potatoes, peas and tomatoes. Keep frying on low heat for ½ hour-45 minutes.

3. Add the *masalas* and salt.

4. Add some butter to the mixture.

5. Garnish with chopped onions and lemon slice.

6. Heat some more butter on a griddle or *tava;* cut *pav* into pieces and heat gently on both sides.

7. Serve the *bhaji* with hot *pav*, finely chopped onions and lemon slice.

Dahi Gunjiya

(Lentil cutlets soaked in curd)

INGREDIENTS

Black gram (*urad dal*), washed	1 cup
Fresh coconut, grated	1½ tbsp
Cashewnuts, chopped	1½ tbsp
Raisins	a few
Oil	for frying
Curd	2 cups
Salt	to taste
Red chilli powder	½ tsp
Cumin seeds (*jeera*), roasted and powdered	½ tsp

METHOD

1. Soak *dal* overnight in water. Grind to a fine paste without adding water.

2. Beat the paste with hand and divide in four parts.

3. Take a wet muslin cloth and spread the *dal* thinly and circularly over it.

4. Put a small portion of grated coconut, nuts and raisins on it.

5. Fold the circle into half to create a *gunjiya*.

6. Deep-fry *gunjiyas* in hot oil till golden brown.

7. Soak *gunjiyas* in lukewarm water till soft.

8. Squeeze out excess water by pressing each *gunjiya* between hands.

9. Beat curd and add salt to it.

10. Immerse *gunjiyas* in curd and serve garnished with red chilli powder and roasted cumin seed powder.

SHAHI TUKDA

(Fried bread slices dipped in cream and sugar syrup)

INGREDIENTS

Bread slices	4
Sugar	1 cup
Water	1 cup
Vetivier (*kewra*) essence	a few drops
Oil	for frying
Milk fat/fresh cream (*malai*)	2 tbsp
Pistachios, chopped	a few

METHOD

1. Mix sugar and water together. Cook till the mixture becomes a little thick. Add *kewra* essence and keep aside.

2. Heat oil in a pan, cut bread slices in circular shapes (alternatively you can use round bread pieces). Fry the slices in oil till golden brown.

3. Soak slices in sugar and *kewra* syrup.

4. Garnish with cream and pistachios. Serve hot.

Alu Tikki
Bhel Puri
Dry White Pea Chaat
Papri Chaat
Stuffed Kulcha
Gulab Jamun

ALU TIKKI

(Spicy potato cutlets served with chutney)

INGREDIENTS

Potatoes, boiled and peeled	4 big
Peas, boiled	½ cup
Bread	2 slices
Salt	to taste
Red chilli powder	½ tsp
Dry mango powder (*amchur*)	½ tsp
Garam masala powder	½ tsp
Green chillies, finely chopped	2
Oil	4 tbsp
Curd, beaten	2 cups
Mint chutney	for garnish
Tamarind chutney	for garnish

METHOD

1. Heat 1 tbsp of oil in a pan. Fry the peas for a few minutes, then add all the spices and green chillies.
2. Soak bread slices in water, squeeze out excess water and mix with the mashed potatoes.
3. Make four balls out of mixture. Flatten one ball on the palm of your hand.

4. Stuff with the peas and spices and close it to make a tight circular flat cutlet once again.
5. Repeat for the remaining balls.
6. Heat a little oil on a *tava*, fry the cutlets (*tikkis*) from both sides till golden brown.
7. Serve hot *tikkis* with plain curd, mint and tamarind chutneys.

BHEL PURI

(Puffed rice mixed with potatoes, onions and spicy masalas served with chutneys)

INGREDIENTS

Puffed rice (*moodi*)	2 cups
Potato, boiled, peeled and chopped	1
Onion, chopped	1
Green chilli, chopped	1
Coriander leaves	a few
Roasted peanuts	2 tbsp
Flat *puris,* broken into pieces	4
Salt	to taste
Chaat masala	½ tsp
Red chilli powder	2 tbsp
Lime juice	1 tbsp
Tamarind chutney	1 tbsp
Mint chutney	1 tbsp

METHOD

Mix all the ingredients and serve immediately.

Note: Puris *for* bhelpuri *are available in the* market.

DRY WHITE PEA CHAAT

(Peas served with hot spices and coriander leaves)

INGREDIENTS

White peas	1 cup
Onion, chopped	1
Green chillies, chopped	2
Lime juice	4 tbsp
Salt	to taste
Soda bi-carbonate	a pinch
Black pepper	1 tsp
Red chilli powder	½ tsp
Garam masala powder	½ tsp
Black salt (*kala namak*)	to taste
Dry mango powder (*amchur*)	½ tsp
Roasted cumin seeds powder	1 tsp
Coriander leaves, chopped	a few

METHOD

1. Soak peas overnight and then boil with a little salt and soda powder.
2. Mix all the ingredients and garnish with chopped coriander leaves and serve immediately.

PAPRI CHAAT

(Crispy flour biscuits served with spicy masalas and chutneys)

INGREDIENTS

FOR DOUGH:

Wheatflour (*atta*)	1 cup
Refined flour (*maida*)	1 cup
Salt	to taste
Carom seeds	½ tsp
Oil	1 tsp

FOR TOPPING:

Onion, chopped	1
Green chilli, chopped	1
Boiled chickpeas	½ cup
Boiled potato, finely chopped	1
Coriander leaves, chopped	2 sprigs
Salt, red chilli powder, roasted cumin seed powder,*chaat masala*	to taste
Tamarind chutney	2 tbsp
Mint chutney	2 tbsp
Sev (*bhujia,* available in the market) (optional)	1 tbsp
Curd	1 cup
Oil	for deep frying

METHOD

1. Mix all the ingredients for the dough, knead well with water and keep aside for half-an-hour.
2. Divide the dough into two parts. Make a big-sized *roti* with each portion. Cut *rotis* into small circles (*puris*) and prick all the mini *puris* or *papris* with a fork.
3. Deep-fry *papris* on slow fire till golden brown.
4. Beat the curd.
5. Dip half of each *papri* in curd and half in tamarind chutney for half a second each.
6. Take them out and place on a serving dish. Put chopped onion, potatoes and boiled chickpeas on the *papris*. Pour the remaining curd, tamarind and mint chutneys as well.
7. Pour all the spices.
8. Garnish with coriander leaves, green chillies and *bhujia*. Serve immediately.

Note: Papris *are also available in the market.*

STUFFED KULCHA

(Fluffy white bread made of flour and milk)

INGREDIENTS

Refined four (*maida*)	1 cup
Oil	for deep-frying
Salt	to taste
Red chilli powder	to taste
Dry fenugreek leaves (*kasoori methi*)	1 tsp
Soda bi-carbonate	½ tsp
Milk	3 tbsp
Dry mango powder (*amchur*)	½ tsp
Onion, chopped	1

METHOD

1. Knead the flour with a little oil, salt, milk and soda powder.
2. Keep aside for half-an-hour.
3. Mix onion, salt, red chilli powder, *amchur* and *kasoori methi* to it.
4. Divide the dough in four parts, roll out each part with a rolling pin and stuff with filling of onion, salt and red chilli powder, close and make a ball. Roll them out again, using a little flour.
5. Deep-fry the rolled out *kulchas* till golden brown and serve with the pea *chaat*.

or

Bake the *kulchas* in an oven. Smear with butter and serve as an accompaniment with spicy *chaats*.

GULAB JAMUN

(Dark brown cottage cheese sweetmeats dipped in sugar syrup)

INGREDIENTS

FOR SYRUP:

Sugar	2½ cups
Water	2½ cups

FOR GULAB JAMUN:

Whole milk fudge (*khoya*), mashed	½ cup
Cottage cheese (*paneer*), mashed	½ cup
Castor sugar	1 tbsp
Refined flour (*maida*)	1 tbsp
Baking powder	a pinch
Oil	for frying
Vetivier (*kewra*) essence	few drops

METHOD

1. Mash and mix the *paneer* and *khoya* to a smooth mixture. Add flour, castor sugar and baking powder.
2. Make a syrup of a thin consistency with sugar and water.
3. Make small smooth balls of the *paneer* mixture (no cracks should appear).
4. Heat oil and deep fry balls on slow fire till they are golden brown in colour.
5. Immerse balls in boiling syrup. Allow to simmer for 7-10 minutes on slow fire. Take care to see they do not break.
6. Remove from fire. Add *kewra* essence and serve hot.

MENU

3

Paneer Moong Dal Chilla
Tandoori Veg
Dahi Kachori
Jhaal Moodi
Kulfi

PANEER MOONG DAL CHILLA

(Cottage cheese and lentil crepes)

INGREDIENTS

Green gram (*moong dal*), washed	1 cup
Salt	to taste
Red chilli powder	½ tsp
Green chillies, chopped	1-2
Garam masala powder	½ tsp
Dry mango powder (*amchur*)	½ tsp
Cumin seeds (*jeera*)	½ tsp
Cottage cheese (*paneer*), grated	½ cup
Coriander leaves, chopped	a spring
Oil	5-6 tbsp
Mint chutney	for garnish
Tamarind chutney	for garnish

METHOD

1. Soak *dal* overnight. Grind in a blender to make a fine paste. Add water for a better consistency.
2. Add salt, red chilli powder, *garam masala* powder and cumin seeds to the mixture.
3. Mix *paneer*, green chillies, salt, *amchur* powder and coriander leaves with this.
4. Heat oil on a griddle (*tava*), spread a spoonful of the *moong* mixture on it, and fry on slow fire, make a filling of the paneer mixture and seal both ends by folding it. Fry till golden brown. Turn to the other side, smear with oil and repeat.
5. Repeat for the rest of the mixture.
6. Serve *chillas* with mint and tamarind chutneys.

TANDOORI VEG

(Barbecued vegetables)

INGREDIENTS

Cottage cheese (*paneer*)	150 gm/10-15 cubes
Capsicum	1
Tomatoes	2
Onions	2
Curd	1 cup
Salt	to taste
Carom seeds	1 tsp
Garam masala powder	1 tsp
Red chilli powder	½ tsp
Chaat masala	1 tsp
Lemon slices	a few
Oil	5-6 tbsp
Gram flour (*besan*)	1 tsp

METHOD

1. Cut all the vegetables and *paneer* into big pieces.
2. Strain the curd. Add salt, red chilli powder, *garam masala* powder, gram flour and carom seeds to it.
3. Marinate the *paneer* and vegetables in it for 3-4 hours.
4. Put them on a skewer, with oil and roast in a *tandoor* oven or a barbecue grill.
5. When the vegetables are brown in colour, sprinkle *chaat* masala on them.
6. Serve with lemon slices, mint chutney and onion rings.

Contemporary Menu 6
Stuffed Brinjal, Vegetable Sticks with Curd dip

Contemporary Menu 7
Broccoli, Baby corn and Mushroom Salad, Mangoodi Matar, Amras and Boondi Raita

Contemporary Menu 9
Mushroom Soup, Tri-Coloured Rice, Fruit Salad

Chaat Menu 1
Pani Puri, Alu Chat, Pav Bhaji and Dahi Gunjiya

DAHI KACHORI

(Fried pancakes with yogurt filling)

INGREDIENTS

FOR DOUGH:

Refined flour (*maida*)	2 cups
Clarified butter (*ghee*)	2 tbsp
Water	to make the dough
Salt	½ tsp

FOR FILLING:

Salt, red chilli powder, garam masala, mango (*amchur*) powders	to taste

METHOD

1. Mix the ingredients for the dough using sufficient water.
2. Leave the dough aside for half-an-hour and knead again.
3. Make small walnut-sized balls from the dough. Roll balls out into flat *puri*-shaped discs, apply *ghee*, sprinkle *masala* for filling on the flat *puris* and close and make circular balls again.
4. Heat oil in a wok, deep-fry balls on slow fire till golden brown. Your *kachoris* are now ready.

FOR ACCOMPANIMENT:

Beaten curd	1 cup
Mint chutney	4 tbsp
Tamarind chutney	4 tbsp
Potato, boiled, peeled and chopped	1
Onion, chopped	1
Green chillies, chopped	2
Coriander leaves	few
Salt, red chilli powder, roasted cumin seed powder and chaat masala	to taste

METHOD

1. Make a depression in the centre of the crisp *kachori* and fill with onion, green chillies and potato.
2. Pour curd, mint and tamarind chutneys on the *kachoris*.
3. Sprinkle salt, red chilli and roasted cumin seed and *chaat masala* powders.
4. Garnish with coriander leaves and serve immediately.

JHAAL MOODI

(Puffed rice chaat)

INGREDIENTS

Puffed rice (*moodi*)	2 cups
Onion, chopped finely	1
Potato, boiled, peeled and chopped	1
Peanuts	2 tbsp
Coconut, grated	2 tbsp
Salt,	to taste
Lime juice	2 tbsp
Red chilli powder	½ tsp
Chaat masala	1 tsp
Oil	½ tsp
Coriander leaves, chopped	2 tsp
Green chillies (optional), chopped	2

METHOD

Mix all the ingredients and serve immediately.

KULFI

(Almond-flavoured icecream)

INGREDIENTS

Milk	4 cups
Cornflour	1 tbsp
Sugar	3 tbsp
Almonds, grated	2
Pistachios, grated	2
Saffron, dipped in a few drops of milk	a few strands
Crushed cardamom seeds	2

METHOD

1. Dissolve cornflour in 1 tbsp of milk and make a paste. Keep aside.
2. Boil the rest of the milk and continue heating till it is half the original volume.
3. Add cornflour paste to it, stirring constantly.
4. Add sugar, cook for a few minutes and remove from fire.
5. Add the grated nuts, cardamom and the saffron (soaked in milk). Pour into conical *kulfi* moulds.
6. Keep moulds in freezer. When set, unmould and serve.

Glossary

TERMS

HINDI	ENGLISH	USES IN INDIAN COOKING
Aam	Mango	The king of tropical fruits, mango is used in desserts and fruit salads.
Adrak	Ginger	Used in chopped or paste form in curries and vegetables. In julienne form, it is a garnish. Dried ginger root is used to flavour pickles.
Ajwain	Carom seeds	Also known as bishop's weed, it is used as a part of batters, as a spice and in savoury dishes.
Aloo	Potato	One of the most widely used vegetable in Indian cooking.
Amchur	Dry mango powder	Used in curries and vegetables for a sour and tangy taste.
Ananas	Pineapple	Used in salads and desserts.
Atta	Wheatflour	Wholemeal flour is used as a base to make different Indian breads.
Badam	Almond	Used as a garnish for sweets and as an ingredient in pulaos and curries.
Badi ilaichi	Black cardamom	Used for flavouring curries and pulaos.
Badiya / Phool hakri	Star aniseed	This dried, reddish-brown fruit, used in small quantities, gives a distinctive aroma to Indian food.
Baingan	Brinjal	A widely used vegetable in Indian cooking; it is mashed with spices to make bharta or in curries.
Bandh gobi	Cabbage	Used in vegetable dishes and also served raw in salads.
Besan	Gramflour	Used as a batter to coat fried savouries/sweets.
Bharwan	Stuffed	Stuffed capsicum, stuffed tomato are common North Indian dishes.
Bhindi	Lady's finger (Okra)	This is a gummy vegetable and should be cooked dry to get best results.

Bhuna hua chana	Roasted chickpeas	Used for making flour or in chutneys
Biryani	None	Rice dish cooked in layers with spicy mutton, chicken or vegetables usually on special occasions.
Chana dal	Bengal gram	This is a form of pulses and is also used to make curries.
Chhena	None	A form of cottage cheese, used as a base for Bengal sweets like *rosogolla* or *rasmalai*.
Chaat	None	Mixed vegetables/fruits made into a spicy savoury dish using a special spice called *chaat masala* and other ingredients.
Chapati /roti	None	Indian bread made with wheatflour. When fried, it becomes a *parantha*.
Chhoti ilaich	Green cardamom	Used as a whole spice, as a part of *garam masala* and in powdered form to flavour sweets and some rice dishes.
Dal	Lentil	In Indian cooking, lentil is boiled with water and turmeric powder and then seasoned with spices. It is an essential part of every meal.
Dahi	Yogurt /curd	Yogurt is added to cooked dishes to make a gravy and is also used as a base for *raitas* and snacks like *dahi vada*.
Dalchini	Cinnamon	Dry sticks which are used to flavour curries, pulaos and as important ingredients of *garam masala*; also used in ground form as a spice.
Dhania	Coriander seeds	Used whole and in the powdered form in curries and vegetables and as a part of *garam masala*.
Dhingri	Mushroom	Usually used in combination with green peas or fresh corn to make exotic dishes. It is added to pulaos too.
Fransbean	French beans	Used in curries and pulaos.
Gajar	Carrot	Used in curries, salads and also desserts.
Gud	Jaggery	A sugar substitute, it imparts a delicate earthy taste to the dish.
Gulab jal	Rose water	Rose water and rose essence are especially used in Indian sweets like *gulab jamuns* and in *sherbets*.

Haldi	Turmeric	Turmeric powder gives a distinctive flavour and colour to curries.
Hara dhania	Coriander leaves	Used as a garnish in several dishes and snacks.
Hing	Asafoetida	A powerful seasoning agent used to flavour curries. Added to curries to give a mild, refreshing, sour taste.
Imli	Tamarind	Tamarind pulp, which can be stored in the refrigerator, is used often in chutneys.
Jeera	Cumin seeds	Used whole or ground, it imparts a spicy, aromatic flavour to curries, pulaos and *raitas*. Light roasting in a dry pan enhances its aroma.
Kabuli chana	Chickpeas	Used in making a North Indian delicacy, *chhole*.
Kaddu	Pumpkin	Used in some curries and also to make a delightful dessert, *halwa*.
Kadhi patta	Curry leaves	Used fresh or dried, they have a warm, appetising aroma and give a delicate spicy flavour to the dish. Used extensively in South Indian cooking.
Kaju	Cashewnuts	Used as a garnish or for decoration in pulaos curries and desserts.
Kala jeera	Black cumin seeds	This spice is used to flavour curries and pulaos especially in North India.
Kala namak	Rock salt	This salt adds its special flavour when added to *chaats*.
Kali Mirch	Black peppercorn	This hot pungent spice is an important ingredient of *garam masala* and often used in curries, rice and savoury dishes.
Kathal	Jackfruit	The raw fruit is used in curries. Its cutlets or *koftas* are especially delicious. Ripe fruits are used to make certain Mangalorean and Konkan sweet dishes.
Kela	Plantain (Banana)	In its raw form, it is used to make *koftas* and in South Indian and Bengali curries. It is also used to make some desserts when ripe.
Karela	Bitter gourd	As the name suggests, this vegetable is bitter but makes tasty preparations. Crisply fried or cooked dry with spices are popular preparations.

Kesar	Saffron	This rare and expensive spice is used in minute quantities to flavour milk-based sweets and sometimes in special curries and *biryanis*. To get maximum flavour, saffron should be dissolved in warm milk for about twenty minutes before use.
Khajoor	Dates	In its dried form, it is used in making sweet and sour chutneys and in desserts.
Khane ka soda	Soda bi-carbonate	Used in making fritters, cakes etc. Also cooks food faster.
Kheera	Cucumber	Used mostly in salads.
Kishmish	Raisins	Used as a garnish in many Indian sweets and in aromatic rice dishes.
Lauki or doodhi	Bottle gourd	This is a watery vegetable used in curries.
Lavang	Cloves	Used as a whole spice to flavour curries. Also in sweets and savouries.
Lehsun	Garlic	Often used whole or in paste form, in combination with ginger, to flavour curries and pickles.
Maida	Refined flour	Used as a base to make different Indian breads and to make snacks.
Makai	Corn	Used in some curries and soups.
Malai	Fresh cream	Used to flavour sweets and some curries. *Malai* can be made at home by cooling boiled milk and skimming off the layer of fat that forms on the surface.
Masala	Spices	Indian cooking uses different kinds of spices such as *garam masala, chaat masala, samhbar masala*.
Masoor	Lentil	Used both as whole and in split form to make thick curries or dals.
Matar	Green peas	These can be used fresh or frozen in curries or pulaos.
Methi	Fenugreek	Fresh leaves are used as a vegetable and in *paranthas*. Dried leaves, known as *kasuri methi* are used for seasoning curries.
Methi dana	Fenugreek seeds	Whole seeds are used for seasoning, whereas the powder is an essential ingredient of pickles. For best results, lightly roast.

Mirch	Chilli	Fresh green/red chillies or red chilli powder are used extensively in Indian cooking to make the food pungent.
Mooli	Radish	Used mainly in salads and to stuff *paranthas*.
Moong	Green gram	Used as whole, sprouted or split (dal). Skinless split gram (*moong dal, dhuli*) is used for making curries and even sweets.
Moong phalli	Groundnut	Used raw or roasted in some curries specially in Maharashtrian and Gujarati dishes.
Narial	Coconut	An important ingredient of South Indian cooking. Its milk and flesh are used in curries, soups, *chutneys*, sweets and as a garnish.
Nimbu	Lime	A citrus fruit used to add tanginess to salads. It also adds a distinct flavour.
Palak	Spinach	This leafy green vegetable is highly nutritious and is used to make curries.
Paneer	Cottage cheese	Used in curries as well as a base in (Indian) sweet dishes.
Papad	None	Thin and spiced lentil discs, usually fried or roasted and eaten as an accompaniment.
Phool Gobhi	Cauliflower	Used in curries and pulaos.
Pyaz	Onion	Chopped or sliced or ground, it is used as a base in many curries and vegetables. Different gravies require different onion pastes. For instance, white gravies require boiled onion paste while red gravies use browned onion paste.
Pista	Pistachio	Used to garnish sweets.
Pudina	Mint leaves	These leaves are widely used in *chutneys* and as a flavouring agent for yogurt. Dried leaves are ground to make mint powder.
Pulao	Pilaff	Rice simmered with vegetables.
Rai / Sarson	Mustard seeds	Whole seeds are used for tempering and in powder or crushed form in pickles.

Raita	None	Yogurt mixed with chopped vegetables or *boondi* (deep-fried corn-sized gramflour balls).
Rajmah	Red kidney beans	A form of pulses and a great source of protein, its curry is a delicacy in North Indian cuisine.
Saunf	Fennel seeds	These dried seeds are used extensively to flavour curries and pickles. They have a sweet aromatic flavour.
Sauth	Ginger powder	This can be used in place of fresh ginger. Popular in Kashmiri food.
Shahad	Honey	Used as a sugar substitute and as a topping.
Shahi jeera	Caraway seeds	Used for flavouring curries and pulaos.
Simla mirch	Capsicum	A vegetable used in salads and in curries.
Sirka	Vinegar	This liquid when added not only gives a sour taste but also adds a distinct flavour. It is used mainly in Goan and Parsi dishes.
Suji /Rawa	Semolina	Used to make Indian breads like *paranthas*, *puris* and as a base in some sweets. Also used in the South for making upma etc.
Tej patta	Bay leaves	Dried leaves are used to flavour curries and rice.
Tikki	None	Cooked mashed vegetables mixed with spices and cooked in a *tandoor* or oven.
Toor /Arhar	Split red gram	Also known as pigeon peas, these in their split form are used to make curries and dals.
Turia	Ridge gourd	Green vegetable; as the name suggests it has ridges and is used in some curries.
Urad (whole)	Black gram	Whole *urad* and *urad* dal are used to make curries. It is also used to make South Indian snacks like *dosa* / *idli* etc.
Kewra	Vetivier	A flower whose essence is extensively used in desserts and *biryanis*.